Sacred Sexuality

Integrating Magic into Intimate Connections

Laura Clarke

Table of Contents

INTRODUCTION

Greetings and welcome to "Sacred Sexuality: Integrating Magic into Intimate Connections," an exploration of the depths of spiritual and human intimacy. This book invites you to investigate the profound and transformational power of sacred sexuality in a world too often marked by haste and surface-level encounters.

Sacred sexuality is fundamentally about going beyond the physical act of making love and exploring the worlds of spirituality, energy, and deep connection. It is an observance of the sacredness ingrained in all facets of our existence, a celebration of the divine within us and our relationships.

Numerous civilizations and traditions have acknowledged the potency of sexual energy as a means of achieving higher states of awareness and spiritual awakening throughout history. Humanity has long honored the mystical power of sexuality, from ancient tantric traditions to indigenous rites honoring the union of male and feminine energies.

As attitudes regarding sex and societal standards continue to change in the modern day, there is a growing movement to restore the sacredness of intimacy. For individuals who want to learn more about holy sexuality and incorporate its life-changing potential, this book is a helpful resource.

With a comprehensive approach to delving into the mysteries of intimacy, "Sacred Sexuality: Integrating Magic into Intimate Connections" draws on insights from spirituality, psychology, and the wisdom of ancient traditions. Every chapter offers helpful advice and perceptive comments to assist you on your journey, covering topics like developing self-love, overcoming past traumas, and managing the difficulties of contemporary relationships.

The idea of magic—a delicate but powerful force that imbues every moment of connection with wonder and reverence—is fundamental to the study of holy sexuality. Accepting the enchantment of close relationships allows us to become vulnerable to deep healing, metamorphosis, and spiritual development.

May this book act as a beacon of light for you as you set out on this journey, whether you are doing it alone or with a partner, leading you to new heights of fulfillment, intimacy, and connection. May you rediscover the holiness of sexuality and become aware of the enchantment in every personal connection as you read through the following pages.

CHAPTER I

Foundations of Sacred Sexuality

Historical Perspectives on Sacred Sexuality

An exciting look into the various ways that human civilizations have understood and respected the close relationship between sexuality and spirituality throughout history is provided by historical perspectives on sacred sexuality. The idea of sacred sexuality has been intertwined throughout religious rites, cultural customs, and philosophical teachings from ancient civilizations to contemporary communities. This reflects humanity's persistent curiosity about the secrets of eroticism, love, and transcendence.

One of the oldest known civilizations, ancient Mesopotamia, placed a high value on sacred sexuality in its reproductive rituals and religious celebrations. As the embodiment of fertility, love, and beauty, the goddess Inanna was one of the pantheon of goddesses worshipped by the Sumerians. Sacred prostitution took place in Inanna-dedicated temples, where priestesses performed sexual rites as a form of worship, signifying the union of the divine and the material world. The deep spiritual significance assigned to sexual energy and its function in the cycle of life and death is highlighted by the belief that these rites would secure the fertility of the land and the prosperity of the community.

In ancient Egypt, the goddess Isis and her companion Osiris were revered as representations of divine love and fertility, exhibiting a similar devotion to sexuality. The story of Osiris's death and resurrection is told in the myth of Isis and Osiris, which goes back to the third millennium BCE. This story represents the never-ending cycle of life, death, and reincarnation. Priests and priestesses engaged in sacred sexual union as a way to invoke the couple's heavenly blessings and ensure the continuation of life in temple ceremonies dedicated to Isis and Osiris. These rites, which demonstrate the ancient Egyptians' profound awareness of the interconnection of sexuality, spirituality, and the natural world, were thought to be necessary for preserving cosmic balance and order.

The ancient Indian books known as the Tantras and Vedas offer significant insights into the spiritual aspects of sexuality. Particularly in Tantra, the spiritual tradition stresses the development of sexual energy as a means of achieving enlightenment and self-realization. Tantra, which has its roots in the idea that all of creation is a manifestation of divine consciousness, teaches its adherents how to use sexual energy to increase their awareness, strengthen their bond with the divine, and enter states of blissful ecstasy. Tantra is a broad term for a variety of techniques, such as breathing exercises, meditation, mantra chanting, and ritualized sexual relations, all of which are intended to awaken the latent Kundalini energy and direct it upward via the chakras in order to attain spiritual illumination.

Perhaps the most well-known ancient Indian treatise on sexuality is the Kama Sutra, which stresses the value of love, dedication, and spiritual connection in close relationships while also providing practical advice on positions, techniques, and erotic arts. The Kama Sutra is a philosophical work that honors the holiness of sensual love and its capacity to transcend the limitations of the physical body and bring lovers together in a state of divine bliss, far from being a simple guide for sexual pleasure. The passage itself states, "In the midst of passion, in the embrace of a lover, I know the joy of life."

Indigenous societies around the world have traditionally revered sexuality as a vital component of life and spirituality. For instance, sexual energy is seen in many Native American tribes as a holy gift from the Creator that should be honored and channeled for the welfare of the individual and the group. The indigenous peoples' profound respect for the interdependence of all living things and the sacredness of the Earth is reflected in the rituals of sacred sexuality they perform to honor their ancestors, call forth fertility, and preserve equilibrium with the natural world.

The veneration of gods like Dionysus, the God of wine and ecstasy, and Aphrodite, the goddess of love and beauty, was one way that the idea of sacred sexuality was expressed in ancient Greece. Rituals of holy sexuality were practiced as acts of devotion and worship in the cults of Aphrodite and Dionysus, which glorified pleasure, ecstasy, and the union of opposites. For instance, the Eleusinian Mysteries were a set of sacred initiation and rebirth ceremonies used by ancient Greek religious rites. Through sexual symbolism and union, participants in these rituals experienced intense levels of ecstasy and divine contact.

As Christianity expanded throughout Europe during the Middle Ages, sexuality-related societal norms saw tremendous shift. The Church made an effort to limit and regulate sexual conduct inside the confines of marriage. But even in the Christian past, there were mystical groups that welcomed holy sexuality as a path to spiritual liberation and unity with the divine, including the Gnostics and the Cathars. Specifically, the Cathars held that sexual union between spiritually matched people may result in the production of a "perfect" soul that would be released from the cycle of reincarnation and bound for union with God.

To sum up, historical viewpoints on holy sexuality present a diverse array of customs, beliefs, and behaviors that have developed throughout the millennia. Sexuality has been regarded as a sacred and transformational power closely linked to spirituality, fertility, and the mysteries of life and death from ancient Mesopotamia to contemporary communities. We can learn a great deal about the various ways that people have viewed and respected the sacredness of sexuality throughout history, as well as how these ideas and practices have shaped our current understanding of spirituality, intimacy, and love, by investigating these historical viewpoints.

Spiritual and Cultural Influences

Examining the complex interactions between spirituality and culture reveals a wealth of customs, beliefs, and practices that have influenced human communities across time. Cultural and spiritual influences are intricately entwined, each profoundly impacting and shaping the other. Spirituality has guided cultural norms, values, and rituals from prehistoric times to contemporary communities. Culture, in turn, has given expression and transmission of spiritual beliefs and experiences a framework.

One of the birthplaces of civilization, ancient Mesopotamia, was deeply impacted by spirituality in all facets of daily life, from politics and the law to art and architecture. For instance, the pantheon of gods and goddesses worshipped by the Sumerians represented various facets of the natural world and the human experience. These deities' temples functioned as hubs of spiritual and cultural activity, where people conducted rites and ceremonies to appease the gods and guarantee the well-being of the neighborhood. The Epic of Gilgamesh, one of the earliest known literary works, reflects the profound spiritual beliefs and understanding of humanity's place in the cosmos held by the Sumerians.

Similar to this, spirituality played a significant role in ancient Egyptian civilization, where the pharaoh acted as both a political and religious figurehead and was seen as a divine go-between between the gods and the populace. The core of Egyptian religion was the veneration of a pantheon of gods and goddesses, each of whom was connected to a particular facet of the natural world and the afterlife. Massive temples and pyramids were built as symbols of religious belief in the afterlife and devotion to the gods, and funeral rites were designed to assure the deceased's passage into the world of the gods.

For thousands of years, spirituality has fueled the advancement of culture and civilization in India. The spiritual and also cultural landscape of the Indian subcontinent has been shaped by the profound insights found in the ancient scriptures of the Vedas, Upanishads, and Bhagavad Gita about the nature of reality, the self, and the universe. The predominant religion in India,

Hinduism, is made up of a wide range of beliefs and customs, including the worship of gods like Vishnu, Shiva, and Devi, as well as the use of yoga and meditation as a means of achieving enlightenment. In Hinduism, the idea of dharma, or duty, is fundamental to understanding one's moral and ethical obligations to society.

Spirituality and cultural traditions like Buddhism, Taoism, and Confucianism have a long history in China, and each offers a different perspective on life and the human condition. Chinese culture and society have been shaped by Confucianism for millennia, which places a strong emphasis on moral development, filial devotion, and social harmony. Conversely, Taoism emphasizes the value of living in balance with nature and views simplicity and spontaneity as means of achieving spiritual enlightenment. Buddhism is a religion that started in India and later extended to China and other areas of Asia. It places a strong emphasis on the virtues of compassion, wisdom, and mindfulness as means of achieving enlightenment and overcoming suffering.

Indigenous civilizations in the Americas have long upheld spiritual practices that are closely entwined with the land, the ancestors, and the natural world. Native American tribes, like the Navajo, Lakota, and Hopi, practice rituals and ceremonies to honor the land's spirits, seek guidance from their ancestors and preserve harmony and balance with the environment. These tribes perceive spirituality as an essential element of daily life. For example, several Native American tribes perform the sacred sweat lodge ceremony as a means of healing, purification, and spiritual rebirth.

In Africa, religious beliefs and customs are intricately intertwined with cultural traditions, exhibiting considerable regional and ethnic variation. Spiritual beliefs are centered around the respect of ancestors, the worship of nature spirits, and the performing of rituals intended to ensure fertility, prosperity, and protection from harm. These beliefs may be traced back to ancient civilizations like Egypt and Nubia, as well as indigenous tribes in sub-Saharan Africa. The interconnection of all living things and the need to maintain harmony and balance with the environment are significant themes in traditional African faiths.

In summary, spirituality has a significant and wide-ranging impact on culture, profoundly influencing people's attitudes, beliefs, and actions. Spirituality has acted as a guiding principle throughout human civilization, from prehistoric times to contemporary societies, shaping the customs, rituals, and cultural norms that constitute its foundation. Understanding the complex interactions that exist between spirituality and culture allows us to appreciate better the range of human experience as well as the ways that practices and beliefs change and adapt over time.

Modern Interpretations and Practices
Examining current spiritual readings and practices reveals a rich and varied terrain molded by the intricacies of modern life and the changing requirements of people looking for connection, meaning, and purpose in their lives. With the rapid growth of technology and the transformation of cultural landscapes in our more globalized world, spirituality has evolved into new forms and manifestations that are influenced by a diverse array of traditions, ideas, and practices. A growing understanding of the interconnectedness of all life and the significance of promoting inner harmony, social justice, and environmental sustainability is reflected in modern interpretations and practices of spirituality, which range from mindfulness meditation to eco-spirituality, from yoga to transpersonal psychology.

In the midst of the fast-paced world of modern existence, mindfulness meditation has become a fundamental spiritual practice, providing people with a potent tool for developing presence, awareness, and inner calm. Mindfulness meditation is a practice that has its roots in the teachings of ancient Buddhism. It entails focusing attention on the present moment, monitoring thoughts and sensations with compassion and curiosity, and developing a spacious and accepting attitude. People who practice regularly have increased emotional resilience, clarity, and insight that help them deal with life's obstacles more calmly and efficiently. Many organizations, including businesses, schools, hospitals, and prisons, have embraced mindfulness training as a way to improve well-being, lower stress levels, and develop a compassionate and understanding culture.

With origins in Buddhism and Hinduism, yoga is another age-old spiritual discipline that has seen a remarkable resurgence in popularity in the modern era. Millions of people practice yoga worldwide to support their spiritual development, mental clarity, and physical well-being. Yoga offers a wide range of techniques for developing strength, flexibility, and mindfulness. It also creates a space for introspection, self-discovery, and spiritual study.

Vigorous vinyasa flow sessions to calm restorative practices are among the options available. Yoga is frequently referred to as a complete self-realization technique that offers practitioners a route to inner tranquility, self-awareness, and spiritual enlightenment in addition to its physical advantages.

A growing movement known as "spirituality," or "spiritual ecology," aims to combine social activism, environmental conservation, and spiritual principles. Ecospirituality is a holistic approach to environmental protection that acknowledges the intrinsic value of all life and the interdependence of humans with the natural world. It draws inspiration from indigenous wisdom traditions, deep ecology, and ecopsychology. The core of the eco-spiritual movement is the practice of nature-based rituals, earth-centered ceremonies, and ecological activism. These practices demonstrate a profound respect for the Earth and a dedication to promoting sustainable and harmonious connections with the environment. Ecospirituality encourages people to develop a sense of connectivity, responsibility, and reverence for the web of life, as well as to acknowledge themselves as essential members of the Earth community.

With its focus on the spiritual aspects of human experience, transpersonal psychology has become a powerful force in today's spiritual environment. It provides insights into the nature of consciousness, personal growth, and the quest for higher states of awareness. Transpersonal psychology examines subjects like mystical experiences, near-death experiences, and states of transcendence, drawing on ideas from both Eastern and Western spiritual traditions. Its goal is to combine spirituality and psychology and advance holistic methods of healing and personal development. Transpersonal psychology encourages people to delve into the depths of who they are and to access the knowledge and strength of their deepest selves. It highlights the significance of self-realization, self-actualization, and self-discovery.

The New Age movement, which first appeared in the latter part of the 20th century, is characterized by a broad spectrum of spiritual teachings, practices, and beliefs that place an emphasis on spiritual awakening, personal development, and empowerment. With a focus on holistic well-being and awareness expansion, the New Age movement includes a wide range of practices like astrology, crystal healing, energy work, and channeling. These practices are influenced by Eastern mysticism, Western esotericism, and alternative healing treatments. Asserting the value of self-actualization, self-realization, and self-discovery, the New Age movement encourages people to delve into their own souls and access the knowledge and strength that reside there. The New Age movement is unified by a shared vision of a society marked by harmony, unity, and spiritual progress, where people are enabled to realize their ultimate potential and awaken to their actual nature despite its diversity and complexity.

In conclusion, current understandings and applications of spirituality encompass a wide range of ideas, practices, and beliefs that have developed in reaction to the intricacies of modern living. People are looking for new approaches to build meaning, purpose, and connection in their lives, and they frequently find inspiration from a wide range of spiritual traditions, beliefs, and practices. These approaches include mindfulness meditation, ecospirituality, yoga, and transpersonal psychology. We may learn a great deal about how spirituality is changing and how it affects people's personal well-being, social transformation, and environmental sustainability in the modern period by investigating these contemporary interpretations and practices.

CHAPTER II

The Magic Within: Understanding Energy and Connection

Exploring the Energetic Dynamics of Intimate Relationships

Examining the energy dynamics of close relationships reveals a deep and complex network of relationships that influence how people behave, speak, and relate to each other. Fundamentally, the idea of energetic dynamics proposes that interpersonal connections are influenced by an imperceptible energy flow between people. This energy can take on multiple forms, such as emotional, physical, or spiritual, and it can significantly influence the dynamics of closeness, reliance, and bonding in a romantic partnership.

The idea of energy resonance is one of the fundamentals of energetic dynamics in close relationships. In relationships, energetic resonance is the phenomenon where people are drawn to each other based on the vibrational frequencies of their energy fields. It is conceptualized similarly to the concept of resonance in physics. Two people are said to be in resonance with one another when their energy frequencies are comparable, which fosters harmony, a sense of connection, and understanding. On the other hand, when people have different energy frequencies, their interactions could be tense, discordant, or conflicting. People can learn more about the dynamics of attraction, compatibility, and relational dynamics in their own relationships by investigating the idea of energetic resonance.

The idea of energy boundaries is another crucial component of energetic dynamics in close interactions. The unseen walls people put up to safeguard their energy, preserve their sense of self, and set appropriate limits in their interactions are referred to as energetic boundaries. These limits, which can be spiritual, emotional, or physical in form, are essential to preserving harmony, balance, and respect for one another in a partnership. People who possess strong and distinct energy boundaries are more adept at articulating their needs, setting limits, and handling difficult situations with compassion and grace. People can develop more self-awareness, self-respect, and self-love in their personal relationships by learning about the idea of energy boundaries.

Examining the idea of energetic exchange also clarifies the manner in which people give and receive energy in interpersonal relationships. Physical contact, energetic resonance, and verbal and nonverbal communication are some of the ways that energy can be exchanged. In partnerships, people feel a sense of reciprocity, mutual support, and emotional connection when they participate in a healthy, balanced, energetic exchange. However, people may feel resentful, depleted, or disconnected when there is an unbalanced or one-sided energetic exchange. People can develop higher degrees of awareness, sensitivity, and mindfulness in their relationships with their partners by studying the dynamics of energetic exchange. This leads to a more profound sense of intimacy and connection.

Furthermore, examining the function of energy healing in close relationships provides an understanding of how people might use energy to resolve disagreements, mend old wounds, and strengthen their bonds with their partners. Energy healing techniques like Reiki, acupuncture, and breathwork operate under the premise that physical, emotional, and spiritual illness can result from imbalances in the body's energy. Through releasing restrictions, reestablishing equilibrium, and encouraging unrestricted energy movement, people can undergo significant self-healing and metamorphosis. People can develop higher levels of intimacy and connection by learning about the role that energy healing plays in intimate relationships. This can help them become more self-aware, empathetic, and understanding of both themselves and their partners.

In addition, studying the idea of energetic alignment clarifies how people might match their energy in relationships with their values, goals, and desires. When people are in harmony with their innermost aspirations, their higher purpose, and their genuine selves, this is known as energetic alignment. People who are energetically aligned feel purposeful, clear, and accurate in their relationships, which enables them to be totally present and genuine in their interactions with their partners. People can develop more profound degrees of intimacy and connection in their relationships by learning to embrace and express themselves more fully through the concept of energetic alignment.

To sum up, studying the energy dynamics of close relationships provides a robust framework for comprehending the unseen factors that influence how people interact, connect, and react to one another. People can develop more awareness, sensitivity, and mindfulness in their interactions with their partners and obtain insight into the underlying dynamics of their relationships by investigating ideas like energetic resonance, boundaries, exchange, healing, and alignment. In the end, people can develop more profound degrees of fulfillment, closeness, and connection in their relationships by studying the energetic dynamics of close partnerships. This will promote more love, harmony, and mutual development.

Techniques for Cultivating Awareness and Sensitivity

Emotional intelligence, meaningful relationships, and personal development all depend on developing awareness and sensitivity. Creating strategies to foster these attributes is more crucial than ever in today's fast-paced, high-stress environment. Whereas sensitivity refers to the capacity to empathize with others, recognize subtle clues, and react compassionately, awareness refers to being in the present moment and tuning in to one's thoughts, feelings, and environment. By developing these abilities, people can forge stronger bonds with others, overcome obstacles in life more skillfully, and enjoy higher levels of contentment and well-being.

Mindfulness meditation is a potent method for developing sensitivity and awareness. Mindfulness is an old Buddhist practice that focuses on accepting, being curious, and being receptive to the present moment. People who regularly meditate can train their minds to become more peaceful, attentive, and focused, which will increase their awareness of their thoughts, feelings, and physical sensations. Research has demonstrated that practicing mindfulness meditation can improve emotional resilience, empathy, and compassion while lowering stress, anxiety, and depression. People can increase their capacity for self-awareness and empathy and create deeper, more meaningful connections with others and themselves by developing daily mindfulness practices.

Journaling is another method for developing sensitivity and awareness. Writing may be a very effective self-reflection method because it gives people a secure, accepting environment in which to examine their ideas, emotions, and experiences. People can discover hidden motives and stressors and develop insight into their patterns, attitudes, and values by journaling on a regular basis. Additionally, journaling can help people get perspective on complex events and manage difficult emotions like grief, rage, or fear. Through writing, people can develop more self-awareness and self-compassion, which improves their understanding of who they are and how they relate to other people.

Another method for developing awareness and sensitivity in relationships is mindful conversation. Being present and actively participating in conversations, speaking with authenticity and respect, and listening intently to others are all components of mindful communication. People can develop empathy, understanding, and trust in their relationships by engaging in mindful conversation, which promotes stronger bonds and respect for one another. In order to respond to others with more clarity, compassion, and insight, mindful communication also entails being conscious of one's own thoughts, feelings, and reactions. People who practice mindful communication can resolve problems more skillfully, forge better bonds with others, and live lives that are more harmonious and connected.

Exercises that include the body, like tai chi and yoga, can also be efficient in developing sensitivity and awareness. These methods, which include mindfulness exercises, breathwork, and gentle movement, assist people in being more aware of their bodies and feelings. People who regularly practice yoga or tai chi can improve their flexibility, strength, and awareness of their bodies, as well as their ability to unwind and feel comfortable. In addition to improving one's physical and mental well-being, these techniques can assist people in releasing tension and stress that has been accumulated in their bodies. People can become more perceptive to their own needs as well as the needs of others by learning to read their bodies' signals and cues. Deeper ties and more meaningful encounters may result from this.

Another good way to develop awareness and sensitivity is to participate in outdoor activities. People can connect with nature and feel a sense of wonder, thankfulness, and amazement when they spend time in it. Be it strolling on the beach, trekking in the mountains, or just lounging in a park, being in nature may assist people in de-stressing, finding inner peace, and reestablishing a connection with both the natural world and themselves. Activities that take place in nature provide opportunities for mindfulness as well since they allow people to fully engage their senses and become totally present in the moment. People can become more conscious of their interconnection with all living things and grow to feel empathy, compassion, and care for the environment by developing a stronger connection with nature.

To sum up, developing awareness and sensitivity is critical for emotional intelligence, personal development, and deep relationships. People can increase their level of self-awareness, empathy, and compassion by integrating methods like body-based practices, journaling, mindful conversation, mindfulness meditation, and outdoor activities into their everyday lives. By developing these abilities, people can forge stronger bonds with others, overcome obstacles in life more skillfully, and enjoy higher levels of contentment and well-being. In the end, people may develop a stronger feeling of connection with others, themselves, and the outside world by developing awareness and sensitivity. This will lead to a life that is more harmonious, compassionate, and understanding.

Connecting with the Divine Within and Without

Seekers and mystics have traveled a long path of self-discovery, spiritual enlightenment, and transcendence in order to connect with the divine both within and without. This path is about acknowledging and paying respect to the divine presence that permeates the world around us, as well as about discovering and using the inherent wisdom, love, and power that each person possesses. People can develop a sense of unity, purpose, and reverence for life by practicing meditation, prayer, ritual, and contemplation. This will help them connect with the divine within and become more aware of the divine presence around them.

Meditation is a very effective technique for opening up to the divine within. In order to meditate, one must calm the mind, concentrate, and become open and receptive to the current moment. Through consistent meditation practice, people can quiet their minds, dispel the illusions of their ego, and feel more deeply connected to their inner selves. People can awaken to the divine presence that exists within them, reach the depths of their existence, and access their intuition and insight through meditation. Through meditation, people can create deeper self-awareness, inner calm, and spiritual fulfillment in their lives by making a connection with the divine inside.

Another effective method for making a connection with the divine, both internally and outside, is prayer. Communicating with the divine through stated words, quiet intentions, or deeply felt emotions is the process of prayer. Through prayer, people can create a greater sense of trust and surrender, express appreciation, open their hearts to the divine presence, and ask for guidance and help. Prayer, whether it is done alone or publicly, has the power to change lives by strengthening one's relationship with God and creating a sense of community among those who are on similar spiritual journeys. People can develop more robust faith, resiliency, and devotion in their lives by praying and connecting with the divine.

Rituals are another potent tool for establishing both an external and inward connection with the divine. Participating in symbolic acts, gestures, and ceremonies that pay homage to the sacred and inspire awe and reverence is known as a ritual. Ritual participation allows people to establish holy space, communicate with the divine, and develop a sense of connectedness with life's rhythms and the cycles of the natural world. Rituals, such as burning candles, reciting mantras, or engaging in sacred dances, have the power to profoundly transform people and awaken their souls while establishing a connection with the divine presence that permeates all of creation. People who participate in rituals can strengthen their relationship with God and develop a feeling of direction, significance, and acceptance in their lives.

Another effective technique for making a connection with the divine, both outside and inside, is contemplation. Contemplation is the process of thinking back on philosophical ideas, sacred writings, and spiritual lessons to enhance one's comprehension of existence's mysteries and the nature of reality. People can develop wisdom, insight, and discernment, as well as strengthen their relationship with the divine intelligence that gives life to everything by indulging in contemplation. Contemplation can be a life-changing activity that strengthens one's relationship with the divine and cultivates awe, wonder, and reverence for the mystery of existence. It can be carried out through reading sacred texts, learning about spiritual teachings, or doing intellectual research. People can develop more clarity, insight, and spiritual awareness in their lives by practicing contemplation.

A voyage of self-discovery, spiritual awakening, and transcendence, connecting with the divine within and without, gives people the chance to strengthen their bonds with both their deepest selves and the outside world. In addition to acknowledging and respecting the divine presence that permeates all of creation, people can access the wisdom, love, and power that are within them by developing practices like meditation, prayer, ritual, and contemplation. By means of these practices, people might develop a sense of oneness, purpose, and reverence for life, as well as awaken to their true essence as divine creatures. In the end, realizing our true selves and the limitless potential we all possess is the path toward establishing a connection with the divine, both within and without.

CHAPTER III

Embracing Your Sacred Self: Personal Growth and Healing

Self-Love and Acceptance as Foundations for Intimacy

Meaningful relationships and healthy intimacy are based on the fundamental pillars of self-acceptance and love. Fundamentally, loving and accepting oneself is accepting who you are with kindness, compassion, and unwavering positive esteem. In order to achieve these, one must develop a strong feeling of internal worth and belonging as well as acknowledge and respect one's strengths, shortcomings, and defects. A strong foundation for intimacy, trust, and connection with others can be established by practicing self-acceptance and love.

Building a positive relationship with oneself is essential to self-acceptance and love. This entails accepting all facets of one's being, including the dark sides that can be challenging to embrace, and treating oneself with care, respect, and compassion. People can learn to support and care for themselves in the same manner that they would a close friend or spouse by engaging in practices like self-compassion, mindfulness, and self-care. People can build resilience, self-assurance, and inner security by cultivating a positive relationship with themselves. This is the cornerstone of building positive relationships with others.

Another crucial element of accepting and loving oneself is self-awareness. Being self-aware entails knowing oneself well and being truthful and genuine with oneself as well as one's needs, wants, and thoughts. People who are self-aware are able to recognize their priorities, values, and boundaries and make decisions that are consistent with who they really are. Recognizing and combating limiting ideas and negative self-talk that compromise one's feeling of value and deservingness of love are further components of self-awareness. People can strengthen their bonds with one another and with themselves by developing self-awareness. They can also make room in their relationships for intimacy, vulnerability, and authenticity.

A vital component of accepting and loving oneself is forgiveness. Letting go of grudges, rage, and guilt toward oneself and others and making the decision to develop empathy and comprehension in their place is the process of forgiveness. People can let go of the emotional burdens that burden them and prevent them from loving and connecting with others and themselves by practicing forgiveness. Acknowledging and respecting one's humanity, accepting that errors and flaws are a part of being human, and deciding to move past them so that you can move forward and learn from them are all necessary components of forgiveness. Through the practice of forgiveness, people can make room in their lives and relationships for recovery, development, and transformation.

Healthy boundary-setting and upkeep are crucial components of self-acceptance and love. In addition to preserving a person's sense of autonomy, agency, and self-respect, boundaries are crucial for safeguarding one's physical, emotional, and psychological well-being. People can establish and uphold a safe and courteous environment in which they and others can freely express their needs, wants, and boundaries. Setting and maintaining limits also entails being aggressive and transparent in communication with people and reciprocating their boundaries. Intimacy, vulnerability, and authenticity can grow in relationships when people establish and uphold appropriate boundaries that promote mutual respect, trust, and understanding.

Another crucial component of accepting and loving oneself is self-care. Setting one's physical, emotional, and psychological well-being as a top priority and making conscious efforts to feed and care for oneself regularly are all parts of self-care. This could be partaking in joyful, fulfilling pursuits like being in nature, expressing oneself creatively, or spending time with close friends and family. Taking care of oneself also entails meeting one's essential requirements, which include eating healthily, exercising frequently, and getting adequate sleep. Healthy relationships with oneself and others are built on a foundation of balance and well-being, which may be attained by engaging in self-care activities. Self-care also helps people manage stress and refuel their energy reserves.

To sum up, good intimacy and meaningful relationships are based on the fundamental pillars of self-love and acceptance. A strong foundation for intimacy, trust, and connection with others can be established by practicing self-acceptance and love. This entails establishing and upholding healthy boundaries, practicing forgiveness, growing in self-awareness, and placing self-care as a top priority. Intimacy, vulnerability, and honesty can flourish in relationships when people embrace themselves with kindness, compassion, and unconditional positive regard. The secret to having meaningful relationships with oneself and other people, as well as to leading a happy, fulfilled life, is ultimately to embrace and love oneself.

Healing Past Wounds and Traumas

In order to promote healing, development, and wholeness in the present, healing previous wounds and traumas entails admitting, processing, and integrating traumatic events from the past. This is a profoundly transformational process. Traumas and wounds can have physical, psychological, or emotional symptoms and can originate from a range of situations, such as early life events, relationships, accidents, or critical life events. These wounds frequently leave behind severe scars that affect people's attitudes, feelings, actions, and interpersonal interactions. They can also make it more difficult for those affected to find happiness, fulfillment, and connection in their life. However, people can start to peel back the layers of shame, fear, and sorrow that have built up over time and start a journey of healing and transformation by partaking in therapeutic activities like therapy, self-reflection, and self-care.

Recognizing the reality of prior traumas and wounds and their effects on one's life is a necessary first step toward recovering from them. This entails facing up to difficult memories, feelings, and ideas head-on and realizing how they have influenced one's worldview, relationships, and sense of self. By opening the way to healing and transformation, acknowledgment enables people to start removing the layers of repression, avoidance, and denial that have kept their wounds hidden deep inside their psyche.

Therapy offers a secure, encouraging environment where people may examine and process their experiences under the supervision of a qualified expert, making it an effective tool for healing old wounds and traumas. In addition to challenging false ideas and perceptions, therapists can assist clients in identifying and unraveling the underlying reasons for their wounds and creating coping mechanisms for handling challenging emotions and triggers. By using techniques like somatic experiencing, EMDR (Eye Movement Desensitization and Reprocessing), cognitive-behavioral therapy, and mindfulness-based methods, people can start to break free from the hold of their prior traumas and develop resilience, self-compassion, and empowerment.

Another crucial component in the healing of prior traumas and scars is self-reflection. In order to gain insight into the patterns, triggers, and dynamics that prolong one's pain and suffering, this entails evaluating one's thoughts, feelings, and behaviors with curiosity and compassion. When used as practical tools for self-reflection, journaling, meditation, and contemplative practices can help people discover their inner landscape, develop a connection with their intuition, and obtain perspective and clarity on their experiences. People can start to unravel the web of unconscious habits and conditioning that have kept them trapped in cycles of pain and suffering by developing self-awareness and self-understanding. This will allow them to take the first steps toward healing and liberation.

Self-care entails putting one's physical, emotional, and psychological well-being first in order to nourish and nurture oneself on a daily basis, which is a crucial component in the healing process from past wounds and traumas. This could be doing things that make you happy, fulfilled, and joyful, including going on walks in the outdoors, creating art, or spending time with close friends and family. Taking care of one's essential requirements, including getting adequate sleep, eating a healthy diet, and also exercising on a regular basis, is another aspect of self-care. People can refuel their energy stores, lower their stress levels, and develop a sense of balance and well-being by engaging in self-care, which lays the groundwork for healing and development.

Since it entails letting go of blame, resentment, and anger toward oneself and others in favor of developing compassion and understanding, forgiveness is a potent tool for healing previous traumas and scars. To be forgiven is to let go of the emotional weight that comes with harboring resentments and grievances, not to support or excuse bad behavior. Through the practice of forgiveness, people can break free from the bonds of the past and allow themselves to be open to the possibilities of recovery, development, and transformation. In order to be able to forgive, one must also be able to acknowledge and respect one's humanity, accept that errors and flaws are a part of being human, and decide to move past them in order to develop and learn.

In the end, overcoming prior traumas and scars is an incredibly intimate and life-changing process that calls for bravery, compassion, and dedication. People can start to remove the layers of shame, guilt, and fear that have kept them caught in cycles of suffering by admitting the existence of their wounds, seeking support through counseling and introspection, engaging in self-care, and forgiving themselves. This may set off a process of recovery and change. People can regain their sense of wholeness, worthiness, and energy, as well as develop increased resilience, self-compassion, and empowerment during this process.

Practices for Cultivating Emotional and Spiritual Wholeness

To experience a profound sense of harmony, fulfillment, and connection with oneself and the world around them, one must nurture and integrate all facets of one's being—body, mind, heart, and spirit—through the transforming process of cultivating emotional and spiritual wholeness. A vast array of activities that support personal development, self-awareness, self-compassion, and a sense of connectedness to something more than oneself are included in the concept of emotional and spiritual wholeness. People can develop resilience, inner serenity, and a strong sense of meaning and purpose in life by consistently partaking in these practices.

Mindfulness meditation is one technique for fostering emotional and spiritual well-being. Rooted in the teachings of ancient Buddhism, mindfulness entails bringing focused attention to the present moment with openness, curiosity, and acceptance. People who practice mindfulness meditation can improve their emotional control, mental clarity, and self-awareness, which will help them deal with life's obstacles more calmly and efficiently. In addition to promoting a stronger sense of self-awareness and awareness of the world around them, mindfulness helps people feel more compassionate, appreciative of life's blessings, and interconnected.

Self-compassion is another technique for developing emotional and spiritual completeness. Self-compassion entails being compassionate, understanding, and accepting of oneself without reservation, especially when facing hardship, sorrow, or failure. By practicing self-compassion, people can become more resilient, accepting, and confident in themselves. They can also learn how to soothe and calm themselves in trying circumstances. As people become more aware of their common humanity and connection to all living things, self-compassion also encourages increased empathy and compassion for other people.

Another effective strategy for fostering emotional and spiritual wholeness is the practice of gratitude. Embracing gratitude entails acknowledging and valuing all of life's opportunities, gifts, and blessings—no matter how minor or seemingly unimportant. People can change their perspective from one of need and scarcity to one of plenty and thankfulness and develop a strong sense of happiness, contentment, and well-being by regularly practicing gratitude. Those who are grateful learn to find beauty and purpose in even the most trying situations, which increases their resilience and optimism.

Another technique for fostering emotional and spiritual balance is creative expression. To express oneself creatively means using one's natural creativity and art, music, writing, or other creative mediums to convey ideas, emotions, and experiences. Through creative expression, people can explore their deepest feelings and thoughts, reach into their unconscious minds, and develop more self-expression, self-awareness, and personal development. By connecting people to the universal source of inspiration and creativity, creative expression also helps people feel more connected to something more than themselves.

Another effective technique for fostering emotional and spiritual wellness is spending time in nature. Awe, amazement, and reverence for the magnificence and interconnectedness of all life may be fostered by spending time in nature. Nature has a tremendous healing and renewing influence on the body, mind, and spirit. People who spend time in nature can feel centered, at ease, and full of energy. Additionally, they can become closer to both their innermost selves and the natural world. Individuals can engage in introspection and contemplation by looking at the natural world, which is replete with life, death, and rebirth cycles.

Performing deeds of kindness and service is another technique for developing spiritual and emotional balance. Serving others is giving of oneself with kindness, understanding, and compassion. It can take many different forms, such as helping friends and family in need or volunteering in the community. People can develop a feeling of meaning, purpose, and connection with others, as well as a deep sense of pleasure and delight by performing deeds of compassion and service. As people become aware of their common humanity and connection to all living things, serving others also helps them develop more profound empathy and compassion for others.

Finally, in order to experience a profound sense of harmony, fulfillment, and connection with oneself and the world around them, nurturing and integrating all facets of one's—body, mind, heart, and spirit—is a transformative journey that goes hand in hand with cultivating emotional and spiritual wholeness. By engaging in creative expression, self-compassion, mindfulness meditation, connecting with nature, and performing acts of kindness and service, people can cultivate resilience, inner serenity, and a profound sense of purpose and meaning in their lives. In the end, pursuing emotional and spiritual wholeness enables people to love fully, live honestly, and accept life as it is—despite any obstacles that may come up in the process.

CHAPTER IV

Rituals and Practices for Sacred Intimacy

Creating Sacred Space: Altars, Symbols, and Sacred Objects

Sacred space creation is a profound and age-old practice that cuts across spiritual and cultural divides. Fundamentally, it entails the deliberate construction of an area, either mental or physical, that is charged with intention, significance, and reverence. Altars, symbols, and holy artifacts are used by people to honor spiritual teachings, develop a more intimate relationship with the divine, and explore their inner selves. By acting as a link between the sacred and the secular, this practice enables people to reach higher states of awareness, knowledge, and understanding.

Altars are places of worship that people make in order to respect and communicate with the divine. They offer a material embodiment of one's spiritual ideas and goals and act as centers for prayer, meditation, and ritual. The size, form, and intricacy of altars can vary greatly; they can be as basic as tabletop displays or as sophisticated as magnificent shrines or sanctuaries. The altar is centered on images or statues of gods, goddesses, or other spiritual entities, as well as symbolic representations of the elements—earth, air, fire, and water. By erecting an altar, people can make their surroundings or homes sacred, bringing the divine in and preparing the ground for spiritual practice and growth.

Symbols are essential to the construction of sacred space because they open doors to more profound levels of comprehension, insight, and significance. Symbols are effective means of connecting with the divine and gaining access to archetypal energies that are not limited by language or cultural boundaries. They can take many different shapes, ranging from personal symbols that have particular meaning for each person to traditional religious symbols like the cross, pentacle, or lotus flower. People can invoke a feeling of connection with the divine and access the collective wisdom and consciousness of humanity by introducing symbols into sacred spaces. Moreover, symbols can work as anchors during introspection and meditation, assisting people in focusing their thoughts and developing their spiritual practices.

Sacred objects are tangible items that people endow with importance and meaning in order to create a sacred environment. Along with ritual implements like incense, candles, bells, or chimes, these objects may include crystals, stones, feathers, shells, or other natural elements. Sacred artifacts can inspire awe, beauty, and harmony in the room while acting as concrete reminders of the sacred. They can also be focal locations for prayer, meditation, and ritual, which can facilitate more significant levels of insight and knowledge and a person's ability to connect with the divine. People who surround themselves with holy items develop a sense of connection with the divine and construct a material picture of their spiritual journey.

Creating sacred space is not just about having tangible items; it's also about developing an attitude of respect, openness, and presence on the mental and emotional levels. This is able to be accomplished through practicing mindfulness, meditation, prayer, or visualization— practices that help people open their hearts, quiet their minds, and tune into the subtle energies of the sacred. No matter where they are, people can achieve a sense of inner serenity, clarity, and connection with the divine by creating a sacred inner space. This inner sacred place offers a haven for introspection, healing, and rejuvenation and forms the basis for spiritual development and transformation.

Sacred space creation is a deeply personal and creative way to express one's relationship with the divine, as well as a potent spiritual practice. It is a chance for people to make a space that fosters their spiritual development and personal journey by adding intention, meaning, and beauty to their surroundings. People can create a space for spiritual discovery, change, and transcendence, as well as nurture a sense of reverence, connection, and harmony in their lives through the use of altars, symbols, sacred artifacts, or inner practices. In addition to experiencing a strong feeling of meaning, purpose, and belonging in their life, people can strengthen their connections with the divine, the world around them, and themselves by honoring the sacred both within and beyond.

Rituals for Deepening Connection and Intimacy

Throughout history, rituals for increasing closeness and connection have been respected in many cultures and traditions. These customs function as sacred rites that promote respect, oneness, and a feeling of interconnectedness among people—whether in love relationships, families, or communities. Fundamentally, rituals are conscious actions carried out with significance and awareness. They are frequently created to commemorate important events, changes, or turning points in a person's life. People can improve their links with others, develop a more profound sense of trust and understanding, and establish a shared sense of meaning and purpose in their relationships by partaking in rituals for increasing intimacy and connection.

Dining together is one of the most popular rituals for increasing closeness and connection. It is well known that sharing food is a potent means of fostering a sense of community and connection with others, as well as nourishing the body and the soul. Eating meals together, whether it's a family meal, a romantic dinner for two, or a group feast, gives people a chance to connect more deeply, tell tales, and come together. People can develop a sense of community and also belonging by eating meals together. They can also make enduring memories and customs that help to fortify their bonds over time.

Expressing thankfulness and appreciation is a powerful ritual for strengthening intimacy and connection. There are many different ways to practice gratitude, ranging from straightforward statements of gratitude to more complex ceremonies or rituals that recognize and celebrate the people and blessings in one's life. People can develop a stronger sense of connection and appreciation for other people and experiences that enhance their lives by taking the time to express thanks and appreciation for one another. Gratitude rituals can enhance the links of trust, love, and understanding in relationships and assist in creating a pleasant and supportive environment.

Another effective practice for increasing intimacy and connection is physical touch. Touch is a global language that expresses love, support, and comfort. It is crucial for building closeness and a sense of connection in romantic relationships. Physical contact, whether it be by holding hands, embracing, or snuggling, can strengthen the ties of affection and love between people by fostering a feeling of warmth and intimacy. People can develop a stronger sense of closeness and connection as well as a secure and supportive environment for emotional expression and vulnerability by including physical touch in their relationships.

Intimacy-building rituals can also entail doing things together or going through experiences that strengthen bonds between people. These can be more sophisticated customs or rituals specific to a relationship or group, or they can be more straightforward daily activities like taking a stroll or watching a favorite movie. People can build their relationships and increase their sense of intimacy and connection with one another by sharing experiences and memories that last a lifetime.

The practice of communicating and active listening is another effective ritual for increasing intimacy and connection. Setting aside time to have frank, sincere, and genuine conversations, as well as to genuinely listen to and comprehend one another's thoughts, feelings, and viewpoints, are all part of communication rituals. People can foster a stronger feeling of empathy, compassion, and understanding in their relationships and establish a secure and encouraging environment for expressing needs, wants, and concerns by engaging in communication and active listening practices. Communication rituals can be used to settle disputes, deepen bonds of love and connection, and promote intimacy and trust in partnerships.

In summary, rituals for increasing closeness and connection are practical activities that can build ties, encourage trust, and give relationships a feeling of cohesion and direction. Rituals offer a means for people to establish enduring memories and customs that enhance their relationships over time. These customs can include sharing meals, expressing gratitude and appreciation, being physically touched, taking part in shared experiences or activities, or practicing communication and active listening. People can develop a more profound sense of intimacy, love, and connection, as well as create a holy place for personal development, healing, and transformation by introducing rituals into their relationships.

Exploring Tantra and Sacred Sexual Practices

Examining Tantra and ritualized sexuality explores historical customs and spiritual routes that see sexuality as a holy and transforming energy. Tantra is a holistic way of living that combines spirituality, sexuality, and personal development. It comes from ancient Hindu and Buddhist traditions. Fundamentally, Tantra acknowledges that every person possesses innate divinity and uses a variety of techniques, such as breathing exercises, meditation, and ritualized making love, to awaken and channel this divine energy. The core of Tantra is the conviction that Kundalini, or sexual energy, is a powerful force that may be used to achieve enlightenment and spiritual awakening.

A fundamental tenet of Tantra is the idea of unity, or the fusion of opposites, which finds expression in the holy sexuality ritual. Those who engage in holy sexual practices do so with a sense of reverence, presence, and intention, with the goal of developing a deeper connection with the divine, their partners, and themselves. These techniques entail developing an attitude of openness, surrender, and mindfulness, as well as letting sexual energy move freely and harmoniously between lovers. People can achieve greater levels of closeness, pleasure, and spiritual awakening, as well as intense sensations of ecstasy, connection, and union, by partaking in sacred sexual activities.

Examining Tantra and sacred sexual practices also involves studying its rituals and ceremonies. Creating a holy space, calling out divine energies, and respecting the divine feminine and male principles inside oneself and one's spouse are standard ritualistic practices. Tantric ceremonies can be as basic as eye gazing or breathwork or as complex as elaborate ceremonies with sacred artifacts, music, and chanting. Through Tantric rituals, people can create a container for profound healing, transformation, and spiritual growth, as well as strengthen their connections with the deity, themselves, and their companions.

Tantra and sacred sexual practices revolve around breathwork, which is a potent technique for gaining access to and circulating sexual energy throughout the body. Conscious breathing patterns are used in tantric breathwork practices to help people relax, open up, and broaden their consciousness. This facilitates the free and harmonious flow of sexual energy throughout the body. People can experience levels of ecstasy and happiness that transcend the boundaries of the ego and the physical body, increase their sensitivity to pleasure, and strengthen their bonds with themselves and their partners by engaging in Tantric breathwork.

Another crucial Tantric and sacred sexuality practice is meditation, which supports the development of presence, attention, and inner awareness in its practitioners. By focusing the mind and turning the attention inward, practitioners of tantric meditation can reach higher states of consciousness and establish a connection with the divine essence that resides inside both themselves and their partners. Through the practice of Tantric meditation, one can quiet the mind, dispel the illusions of the ego, and gain a deep sense of unity and oneness with everything that exists. The development of inner serenity, self-awareness, and clarity—all necessary for negotiating the challenges of close relationships and spiritual awakening—is another benefit of meditation.

Tantra-based sacred sexuality emphasizes the development of a profound and profound connection with oneself, one's partner, and the divine rather than only physical pleasure or enjoyment. It is a route of personal development and spiritual awakening that gives people the chance to discover and embrace their sexuality in a sacred and life-changing way. Through the practice of sacred sexual rituals and the acceptance of Tantra's teachings, people can access an extensive reservoir of sexual energy inside themselves that can be used for spiritual awakening, healing, and transformation. People can strengthen their bonds with the divine, their lovers, and themselves by engaging in practices like breathwork, meditation, sacred sexuality, and Tantric rites and ceremonies. They can also create a sacred space in their lives for significant healing, transformation, and spiritual advancement. In the end, Tantra encourages people to accept their innate divinity and become aware of the limitless potential that each person and every connection has.

CHAPTER V

Navigating Challenges and Celebrating Diversity

Communication and Consent in Sacred Relationships

Consent and communication are fundamental elements of any relationship, but in sacred relationships—where physical, emotional, and spiritual energies come together —they are especially important. Within the context of holy partnerships, people work to develop strong bonds, mutual respect, and spiritual development with their partners. These relationships are based on effective communication, which promotes intimacy, understanding, and empathy. A sense of trust and safety is fostered in relationships when partners are able to express their needs, wants, and boundaries via open and honest communication. This communication weaves a complex web of understanding and connection that goes beyond words to encompass body language, nonverbal clues, and energetic exchanges.

Another essential component of holy connections is consent, which guarantees that all interactions are undertaken voluntarily, joyfully, and with complete knowledge and comprehension. Consent in sacred relationships includes a profound respect for each person's autonomy, agency, and sovereignty in addition to being an agreement to engage in sexual action. In holy partnerships, partners respect each other's limits, needs, and desires and work to foster an atmosphere in which they both feel free to freely express their wants. Active communication, respect for one another's wants and preferences, and mutual awareness are all necessary for the continuous process of consent.

Consent and communication in sacred relationships are dynamic activities that develop and deepen over time rather than static conceptions. Partners always work to learn more about each other and themselves, developing vulnerability, empathy, and compassion in their relationships. They establish a welcoming environment that fosters open communication so that people can share their wants, worries, and insecurities without worrying about being rejected or judged. In sacred partnerships, partners create a strong link of trust and intimacy via this process of communication and consent, where they feel seen, heard, and appreciated for who they really are.

Active listening is one of the most important components of good communication in holy partnerships. Active listening means paying close attention to what the other person is saying, comprehending it completely, and not interjecting, passing judgment, or pushing one's own agenda. To really comprehend another person's point of view, one needs patience, empathy, and the ability to set aside one's own. In sacred relationships, active listening allows partners to validate each other's experiences, emotions, and viewpoints while also creating a space for deep connection and understanding.

The capacity for aggressive and genuine self-expression is a crucial component of communication in holy relationships. This entails having the ability to politely, directly, and precisely express one's needs, wants, and boundaries. Partners can respect each other's wants and boundaries while still advocating for themselves and their needs when they communicate assertively. It fosters an atmosphere of equality and respect between the partners, enabling them to communicate freely and honestly with one another.

In sacred relationships, consent entails recognizing each other's emotional and spiritual boundaries in addition to their physical ones. This entails acknowledging and honoring one another's requirements for privacy, independence, and self-care as well as abstaining from pressing or forcing one another into endeavors or situations they find uncomfortable. In sacred relationships, consent is an ongoing process of mutual agreement, communication, and negotiation in which both partners actively contribute to co-creating a loving, respectful, and empowered connection for themselves.

To sum up, permission and communication are crucial elements of holy partnerships because they lay the groundwork for a close bond, mutual trust, and intimacy. Open, sincere, and compassionate discussion is necessary for effective communication because it gives partners the confidence and security to express themselves honestly and assertively. Respecting each other's autonomy, boundaries, and wishes is the foundation of the continuous process of negotiation and agreement that is known as consent. People may establish a holy place where love, respect, and understanding bloom and where both partners feel free to express themselves fully and authentically by practicing communication and consent in their relationships.

Overcoming Obstacles and Blockages

Overcoming barriers and setbacks is a necessary aspect of the human experience as people work through the intricacies of relationships, life, and personal development. Blockages and obstacles can take many different forms, such as mental difficulties, emotional trauma, physical difficulties, and spiritual crises. These barriers, which can prevent people from living fully and truthfully, can be caused by karmic patterns, limiting beliefs, cultural conditioning, or past experiences. People may, however, overcome these challenges and recover their power if they are conscious, resilient, and determined. In the process, they will experience greater freedom, fulfillment, and wholeness.

Being conscious of and accepting that there are hurdles and impediments in one's life is one of the first steps toward conquering them. Being aware of oneself entails adjusting one's thoughts, feelings, and also behaviors as well as recognizing any patterns or triggers that might be causing the problem. People can acquire clarity and insight into the underlying reasons for their challenges and start to comprehend how they are affecting their lives by engaging in self-reflection, introspection, and mindfulness exercises.

After raising awareness, people can start looking into ways to go through their barriers and challenges. This can entail asking for help from loved ones, friends, or mental health specialists, who can provide direction, inspiration, and insight. It could also entail self-care activities like journaling, yoga, or meditation, which support the development of resilience, self-awareness, and emotional control in people. In addition, people might look into complementary and alternative forms of treatment, including bodywork, energy work, or shamanic rituals, which can aid in the release of energetic blockages and more profound forms of healing.

An additional crucial component of getting beyond barriers and impediments is accepting and facing discomfort. People who want to grow and evolve frequently have to get out of their comfort zones and face their fears, insecurities, and limits. People can develop inner strength, bravery, and resilience, as well as increase their potential for personal development and self-discovery by accepting the difficulties that come with embracing discomfort. This could entail attempting new things, taking chances, or facing challenging feelings or circumstances—all of which have the potential to produce essential realizations and breakthroughs.

To overcome barriers and setbacks, people must practice self-compassion and forgiveness because it enables them to let go of their shame, guilt, and self-judgment and to accept and love who they are. In order to be self-compassionate, one must treat oneself with the same consideration, empathy, and kindness that one would extend to a friend in need and acknowledge that difficulty and imperfection are inherent aspects of being human. People can heal old traumas, build resilience, and increase their sense of self-worth and self-love by engaging in self-compassion practices. These abilities are crucial for thriving in life and overcoming problems.

Cultivating a growth mindset—the conviction that difficulties and failures present chances for learning, development, and self-improvement—is another essential component in overcoming barriers and locations. Instead of approaching challenges with defeatism or resignation, those with a development mindset can approach them with curiosity, hope, and tenacity. By reinterpreting barriers as chances for development and change, people can change their viewpoint and give themselves the confidence to conquer even the most difficult tasks. This entails accepting failure as an inevitable component of learning and seeing obstacles as transient rather than unbreakable.

Connecting with a higher power and also engaging in spiritual activities can be effective strategies for getting past roadblocks and hurdles. Prayer, meditation, and ritual are just a few of the techniques that many spiritual traditions offer to aid people in developing their faith, submission, and confidence in a greater force or universal intelligence. People may find courage, direction, and support in managing life's difficulties and conquering barriers by giving up control and putting their faith in a greater force. Additionally, spiritual activities provide people with a feeling of direction, significance, and perspective that enables them to see beyond their own challenges and establish a connection with something bigger than themselves.

In summary, overcoming barriers and impediments is a process of self-knowledge, development, and transformation that calls for bravery, resiliency, and awareness. By being more self-aware, seeking support, enduring discomfort, cultivating self-compassion, embracing a growth mindset, and connecting with a higher force, people can overcome even the most formidable challenges and reclaim their power and agency in their lives. Through this process, people can start down a path of healing, growth, and self-realization and discover greater freedom, fulfillment, and wholeness.

Honoring Diversity in Sexual Orientation, Gender Identity, and Expression

Respecting differences in gender identity, sexual orientation, and expression is a fundamental acknowledgment of the complexity of the human experience and identity. It means creating inclusive settings where people are appreciated, valued, and celebrated for who they indeed are, irrespective of their gender identity, sexual orientation, or preferred mode of self-expression. The necessity of respecting diversity in various domains will be discussed in this section, along with the difficulties LGBTQ+ people encounter, the value of advocacy and allyship, the intersections of identities, and the steps communities may take to make their spaces more inclusive.

A range of attraction is referred to as sexual orientation, which includes heterosexuality, homosexuality, bisexuality, pansexuality, asexuality, and more. It is a fundamental component of who they are and has the power to affect many facets of life, including interpersonal and social connections. In order to honor the diversity of sexual orientation, one must acknowledge that there is no one "normal" or "right" way to feel attraction and must instead acknowledge and accept the validity of all orientations.

In a similar vein, gender identification refers to an individual's internal sense of gender, which may or may not match the sex to which they were biologically assigned. Transgender, nonbinary, genderqueer and genderfluid identities are among the spectrums of gender identity. Respecting the multiplicity of gender identities means utilizing each person's preferred name and pronouns while also honoring their self-identified gender.

The external representation of a person's gender identification, such as attire, haircuts, body language, and other cultural indicators, is referred to as gender expression. Creating environments where people may express themselves freely and authentically without worrying about discrimination or judgment based on societal standards or expectations is essential to honoring variation in gender expression.

The difficulties LGBTQ+ people encounter are prejudice, assault, stigma, and discrimination. LGBTQ+ people may encounter obstacles when trying to get housing, work, healthcare, and other necessities because of their gender identity or sexual orientation. They could also encounter animosity or rejection from classmates, family, religious groups, or society at large, which can result in internalized homophobia or transphobia as well as feelings of loneliness and humiliation.

For LGBTQ+ people to live in inclusive and supportive contexts, activism and allyship are essential. People who actively support and promote for LGBTQ+ rights and equality are known as allies. They use their power and influence to confront prejudice and discrimination. Raising awareness, encouraging acceptance, and establishing safer environments for LGBTQ+ people to live, work, and prosper are all essential tasks that allies may undertake.

When talking about diversity in gender identity, expression, and sexual orientation, intersectionality is crucial to take into account. Intersectionality recognizes that people have numerous identities and that, in addition to their LGBTQ+ identification, they may experience overlapping forms of oppression or discrimination based on criteria like color, ethnicity, class, disability, or immigration status. It is imperative to acknowledge and tackle these interlocking structures of subjugation in order to establish genuinely fair and inclusive environments for every person.

By putting in place inclusive policies and practices, offering education and training on LGBTQ+ issues, cultivating supportive networks and resources, and amplifying LGBTQ+ views and perspectives, communities can seek to honor variety in sexual orientation, gender identity, and expression. Through proactive efforts to provide settings that are inclusive, affirming and value variety, communities can lessen stigma, encourage acceptance, and enhance the well-being and standard of living for LGBTQ+ people and communities.

In summary, valuing diversity in sexual orientation, gender identity, and expression is essential to building egalitarian and inclusive communities where people of all backgrounds are accepted, appreciated, and celebrated for who they are. Communities can create a world where everyone can live authentically and openly, free from fear, stigma, and discrimination, by recognizing and affirming the validity of diverse sexual orientations and also gender identities, challenging discrimination and prejudice, fostering supportive allyship and advocacy, acknowledging intersectional identities, and working towards creating more inclusive spaces. We can create a more compassionate and also just society where variety is valued and appreciated as a source of resilience and strength by working together and showing solidarity.

CHAPTER VI

The Sacred Union: Partnership and Beyond

Exploring Sacred Partnership and Soul Connections

Examining soul connections and sacred partnerships allows one to dive into the profoundly transformational nature of relationships that go beyond the typical definitions of companionship and love. The awareness of a profound spiritual connection between people, marked by respect, understanding, and unwavering love, is the fundamental component of holy partnership. Sacred partnerships, in contrast to ordinary romantic relationships, are founded upon a more profound sense of purpose and soul resonance, where two souls come together to assist each other's growth, evolution, and spiritual journey. These relationships may be based on attraction, compatibility, or common interests.

Those who feel drawn together by a higher force or global intelligence are guided in sacred partnerships by a sense of divine alignment. This connection accesses the natural wisdom and knowing of the soul, transcending the confines of ego and personality. In sacred partnerships, people acknowledge one another as spiritual partners or soul mates, united by a common purpose or destiny that transcends place and time.

The idea of soul contracts, or agreements, which are planned agreements made between souls before incarnating into physical bodies, is central to the concept of sacred partnership. These contracts specify the roles people will play in each other's lives as well as the lessons, opportunities for growth, and experiences people will have throughout their lives. Those in sacred connections frequently have a feeling of familiarity or deja vu when they instantly recognize and resonate with one another as though they have known one another for many lifetimes.

Those who participate in sacred partnerships are expected to go deeply into their souls and pursue self-discovery, as well as to present themselves as really vulnerable. These connections act as mirrors, reflecting back to people both their greatest assets, talents, and potential as well as their most profound scars, anxieties, and insecurities. People are asked to recover from previous traumas, let go of limiting beliefs, and accept their actual nature and strength through this mirroring process.

As people work to establish an environment of trust, transparency, and authenticity in their relationships, communication is a fundamental component of sacred partnerships. This entails having in-depth, meaningful discussions in which people encourage one another's personal development and evolution while sharing their ambitions, dreams, anxieties, and aspirations. Sacred partnerships weave a complex web of knowledge and connection through nonverbal clues, energetic exchanges, and intuitive knowing, in addition to vocal communication.

Sacred partnerships are with difficulties as partners work through the intricacies of their interpersonal dynamics and their own inner terrain. These difficulties could be caused by emotional scars from the past, intimacy anxieties, or behavioral habits from past encounters. But in sacred partnerships, people lean into discomfort and face their shadow sides with compassion and courage, viewing obstacles as chances for personal development and healing.

In sacred partnerships, forgiveness and compassion are vital traits that help people through the highs and lows of their relationship. To be forgiven is to let go of grudges, accusations, and condemnations directed at oneself and other people, as well as to adopt an attitude of empathy and comprehension. People who forgive themselves and their partners are able to move past their past hurts, restore damaged relationships, and develop more profound empathy and connection.

Spiritual activities like prayer, meditation, and ritual can strengthen the ties that bind people in sacred partnerships and offer a framework for development, transformation, and connection. Through these exercises, people can strengthen their relationships with God, their partners, and themselves, as well as develop presence, mindfulness, and inner awareness. People can establish a holy place for intimacy, healing, and spiritual awakening in their relationships by integrating spiritual activities.

In conclusion, people can strengthen their bonds with the divine, their partners, and themselves by delving into the themes of sacred partnership and soul connections. People are able to form relationships that facilitate their spiritual development, evolution, and growth when they are characterized by mutual respect, understanding, and unconditional love. People can build relationships based on love, purpose, and spiritual connection by adopting the principles of sacred partnership, which include soul contracts, divine alignment, genuine communication, forgiveness, and spiritual practice. People can go through a road of greater significance, fulfillment, and joy, as well as significant healing, change, and spiritual awakening through the journey of sacred partnership.

Nurturing Intimate Bonds: Love, Trust, and Respect

Building close ties involves a profound journey that includes teaching partners to love, trust, and respect one another. Love is the fundamental element of personal relationships; it is a powerful, transforming energy that unites people in a profoundly loving and connected way. Acts of kindness, care, and compassion are ways that love is conveyed. Physical affection, emotional support, and quality time are ways that love is nurtured. Building close relationships teaches people to be completely honest and vulnerable with one another as they navigate the highs and lows of life together.

Since trust serves as the cornerstone of all relationships, it is also crucial for fostering personal ties. Trust entails having confidence in a partner's dependability, honesty, and integrity, as well as feeling safe in knowing that they will act in your best interests. Honesty, transparency, and regular communication are all essential components of building trust. Reliability, accountability, and boundary respect are other essential components. Healthy personal relationships help people become more self-aware, intuitive, and perceptive and teach them to trust not just their spouse but also themselves.

The third pillar of developing close relationships is respect, which includes a profound regard and admiration for one's partner as a unique and valued person. Respect entails appreciating and respecting one another's viewpoints, beliefs, and boundaries, in addition to upholding one another's autonomy, agency, and dignity. In order to build a relationship built on equality, mutual support, and shared ideals, people work to develop empathy, compassion, and sensitivity to each other's needs and feelings through personal bonding.

Intimate relationships require open and honest communication for people to express their needs, wants, and feelings, as well as for others to listen to them with compassion and understanding. Active listening, validation, and the capacity to respectfully and assertively express one's own needs, desires, and boundaries are all necessary for effective communication. Building close relationships teaches people how to communicate authentically and compassionately, which strengthens intimacy, connection, and trust in a partnership.

Any relationship will inevitably have conflict; therefore, developing the ability to handle it constructively is crucial to fostering close relationships. In addition to unfulfilled wants, unresolved emotions, and old scars, conflict can also result from disparities in values, beliefs, or expectations. People who have intimate, solid relationships learn how to handle disputes by being open-minded, curious, and willing to hear each other out. They look for mutually beneficial solutions that respect the needs and sentiments of both parties in order to settle disputes amicably and cooperatively.

In order to develop compassion, empathy, and understanding toward one another, as well as to let go of hurt, resentment, and anger, forgiveness is a necessary component of maintaining close relationships. In order to be forgiven, one must choose to show grace and mercy to their spouse despite hurt or betrayal and let go of the drive for vengeance or retaliation. People who cultivate close relationships learn to forgive not just their spouse but also themselves, realizing that forgiveness is a necessary step on the road to recovery and a doorway to more intimate and meaningful relationships.

Another aspect of fostering close relationships is spiritual connection, which entails realizing each other's divine presence and establishing soul-to-soul connections. A sense of purpose and meaning in life, along with shared values, beliefs, and practices, are all components of a spiritual connection. In order to foster close relationships, people engage in meaningful discussions about spirituality, life's mysteries, and practices like prayer, meditation, or ritual that help them explore and develop their spiritual connection.

In summary, maintaining close relationships is an intense journey that includes love, trust, and respect and calls on both partners to be committed, patient, and dedicated. People can build a robust and enduring bond that enhances their lives and gives them happiness, fulfillment, and purpose by practicing love, trust, and respect in their relationships. Intimate relationships based on vulnerability, authenticity, and mutual support can be fostered by individuals through spiritual connection, constructive conflict resolution, good communication, and forgiveness. These bonds also bring out the finest qualities in both partners. People who cultivate close relationships go on a path of personal development, recovery, and metamorphosis and establish genuinely sacred and uplifting relationships.

Balancing Independence and Interdependence

In relationships, people must dance delicately between independence and interdependence in an effort to strike a balance between connection and autonomy. While interdependence entails relying on and supporting others as well as sharing respect, trust, and cooperation, independence is the capacity to make decisions, pursue goals, and accept responsibility for one's own life. Achieving equilibrium between these two facets is crucial for constructing wholesome and satisfying connections that nurture development, closeness, and reciprocal assistance.

Independence enables people to develop a sense of agency, self-reliance, and self-esteem, which is a crucial component of self-empowerment and personal development. It entails being aware of oneself, establishing limits, and pursuing one's own passions, interests, and objectives without regard to outside pressures or influences. Being independent also means accepting responsibility for one's feelings, ideas, and deeds, as well as accepting responsibility for the decisions one takes in life. Independence in partnerships enables people to contribute to the partnership from a position of strength and confidence while simultaneously preserving their feeling of autonomy and uniqueness.

On the other hand, placing too much focus on independence can cause loneliness, alienation, and a lack of closeness in relationships. Tension, resentment, and conflict can arise in a relationship when people put their own needs and wants ahead of their partner's. Additionally, people may be afraid of losing their identity or being overly reliant on their spouse, which might keep them from opening themselves completely and developing a deeper connection. A good, long-lasting partnership that respects the interests and preferences of both parties requires striking the correct balance between independence and interdependence.

Conversely, interdependence entails appreciating and acknowledging the interdependence of all creatures and the significance of relationships in influencing our lives. It entails sharing respect, trust, and cooperation with others as well as depending on and helping others. People who are interdependent can share their lives with others, rely on one another for support and direction, and go through life's problems and successes together. Interdependence in a relationship makes people feel appreciated, understood, and supported by their spouse, which promotes closeness, connection, and emotional stability.

Overemphasizing interdependence, however, can result in codependency, a condition in which people depend unduly on their spouse for happiness, validation, and self-worth. In an attempt to satisfy their partner or keep the connection going, people in codependent relationships may lose sight of their own wants and desires, which can be characterized by entanglement, control, and a lack of appropriate boundaries. A partnership built on equality, respect, and trust where both partners feel free to express who they really are and follow their own interests and ambitions requires striking the correct balance between independence and interdependence.

Effective communication is crucial to achieving a balance between independence and reliance in relationships because it allows people to negotiate and navigate the complexities of partnership with empathy and understanding, as well as to openly and honestly express their wants, desires, and boundaries. People who communicate well together can work through issues, discover common ground, and co-create a partnership that respects the autonomy and connectedness of both parties. Furthermore, engaging in active listening, empathy, and validation practices can support people in developing a more profound comprehension of their partner's viewpoint as well as increase closeness and trust in their relationship.

Setting limits enables people to respect their partner's wants and preferences while simultaneously preserving their sense of self and autonomy, which is another crucial component of striking a balance between independence and reliance in relationships. Setting limits helps people feel less overwhelmed or suffocated by their partner's expectations and demands, and it also helps foster a sense of safety, stability, and predictability in the relationship. A solid and long-lasting relationship that promotes development, closeness, and respect for one another can be established by persons who establish and uphold boundaries.

In summary, people negotiate this dynamic and continuous process of balancing independence and interdependence in their relationships in an effort to strike a balance between connection and autonomy. Healthy and satisfying relationships that respect the needs and desires of both partners can be established by individuals through practicing empathy and understanding, setting boundaries, speaking effectively, and developing a strong sense of self and identity. Individuals can achieve a really fulfilling and life-affirming partnership by achieving more intimacy, connection, and fulfillment in their relationships through the process of balancing independence and interdependence.

Embracing Sacred Partnership and Interdependent Connections

A comprehensive approach to partnerships that values the relational, spiritual, and emotional aspects of human connection is referred to as sacred partnership. It entails developing a profound sense of awe, respect, and dedication for oneself, one's spouse, and the relationship as a whole. Sacred partnerships are defined by shared values and objectives, mutual support, and a shared commitment to personal development. They offer an environment that is loving and supportive for both individual and group development, enabling partners to discover and express who they really are and to develop and grow in harmony and respect for one another.

Conversely, interdependent connections entail acknowledging and respecting the intrinsic interdependence of all life as well as the interconnection of all beings. Interdependent relationships acknowledge that we are all a part of a wider cosmic web of life, transcending the ego-centric idea of separateness. They entail developing empathy, compassion, and a sense of solidarity with others, as well as realizing how closely our well-being is linked to that of others and the environment. Building more harmonious, equitable, and long-lasting relationships and communities is made possible by interdependent connections, which also enable us to collaborate on shared objectives and ambitions.

Adopting interdependent relationships and holy partnerships has its challenges, though. Building solid and meaningful relationships can be difficult in a society that frequently places a higher value on individualism, rivalry, and self-interest. Furthermore, people may experience internal obstacles that prevent them from thoroughly engaging and connecting with others, such as a fear of intimacy, abandonment, or vulnerability. Furthermore, external obstacles like societal conventions, cultural expectations, or institutional inequities could make it more difficult for them to establish and preserve deep relationships with other people.

Developing a sense of vulnerability, openness, and authenticity in our relationships is crucial if we are to accept holy partnerships and interdependent connections. This could entail engaging in activities like self-analysis, dialogue, and active listening that support the development of our emotional intelligence and self-awareness and enable us to communicate our needs, wants, and limits in a compassionate and transparent manner. It also entails developing closeness and trust with our partners via deeds of generosity, understanding, and encouragement, which enables us to provide a secure and supportive environment for development and discovery.

Furthermore, recognizing interdependence and holy collaboration necessitates a dedication to relationships and personal development. This could entail doing exercises like mindfulness, meditation, or counseling that assist us in letting go of limiting beliefs, healing past traumas, and developing a stronger sense of self-acceptance and self-love. In order to strengthen our intimacy and connection with our partners and to promote more empathy and understanding in our interactions, it also entails trying out novel approaches to relationships and communication.

In addition, accepting sacred partnerships and interdependent relationships necessitates a dedication to social justice, equity, and inclusiveness, as well as an understanding of the intrinsic dignity and worth of all living things. This could entail opposing repressive institutions, tearing down unfair systems, and pushing for laws and procedures that uphold human dignity and social equality. Our contact with others also entails cultivating empathy, compassion, and solidarity, which enables us to forge understanding and collaboration beyond barriers of difference and division.

In summary, accepting sacred partnerships and interdependent ties presents a life-changing chance to develop profound, meaningful connections marked by trust, respect, and interdependence. We may create a space for personal and relational growth and transformation by treating our interactions with reverence and sincerity. This will enable us to grow and thrive together in harmony and mutual respect. We may access a tremendous reservoir of healing, development, and transformation that enlivens our lives and satisfies our hearts when we accept holy collaboration and interdependent connections.

CHAPTER VII

Sacred Sexuality in Everyday Life

Integrating Sacred Practices into Daily Routines

A potent method of giving daily life meaning, purpose, and a spiritual connection is to incorporate religious practices into routines. Rituals, habits, or pursuits that have significant personal meaning and resonance and foster a sense of oneness with the divine, the cosmos, or one's higher self are referred to as sacred practices. Depending on individual beliefs, customs, and tastes, these practices can take many different forms, but they frequently incorporate aspects like prayer, meditation, mindfulness, gratitude, and introspection. People can experience more harmony, balance, and fulfillment in their lives, as well as a sense of sacredness and reverence in even the most routine activities, by implementing holy practices into their daily lives.

Prayer, which is speaking with a higher power or divine presence with words, thoughts, or intentions, is one of the most famous sacred rituals. There are many different ways to pray: you can say silent prayers while meditating, or you can say formal prayers aloud from sacred texts. Whatever its form, prayer gives people a sense of guidance, comfort, and connection. It also enables them to express appreciation, ask for help when they need it, and seek advice. People can find more serenity, meaning, and spiritual connectedness in their lives and develop a closer relationship with God by making prayer a regular part of their daily routines.

Another potent spiritual practice that can support people in developing awareness, presence, and inner calm is meditation. In meditation, the mind is stilled, attention is directed toward the breath, and thoughts and sensations are noted objectively. People who meditate on a daily basis can improve their emotional control, mental clarity, self-awareness, and sense of connectedness to both the outside world and themselves. People can feel more balance, peace, and well-being in their lives, and they can create a holy place for introspection, regeneration, and spiritual development by incorporating meditation into their daily routines.

Developing an attitude of appreciation and thankfulness for the blessings and gifts in one's life is the spiritual practice of gratitude. Saying "thank you" to people, maintaining a gratitude notebook, or just pausing to notice the wealth and beauty of the current moment are all examples of practicing thankfulness. People can change their perspective from one of scarcity and lack to one of excess and abundance and enjoy more joy, fulfillment, and contentment in their lives by frequently practicing thankfulness. By including appreciation in everyday activities, people can develop a more upbeat mindset, strengthen their sense of self and other-connectedness, and feel happier and more resilient when faced with obstacles in life.

Another holy practice is reflection, which is giving oneself time to think over and learn from one's thoughts, feelings, and experiences. There are various ways to reflect, such as keeping a journal, spending time alone in thought, or having deep discussions with other people. People can improve their understanding of themselves and the world around them and obtain clarity, perspective, and direction in their lives by making frequent time for contemplation.

In addition to facilitating emotional processing and conflict resolution, reflection can help people develop more vital self-awareness and empathy, which can result in more meaningful interactions and connections with others.

To respect the divine and foster a sense of sacredness in their homes, people may also include additional sacred rituals or routines into their daily lives, such as lighting candles, burning incense, or building altars. People can experience more connection, meaning, and purpose in their daily activities and establish a sense of ritual and reverence in their lives by implementing these practices into their daily routines. Adding sacred practices into daily routines can help people experience a more profound sense of connection with themselves, others, and the divine, as well as greater spirituality, presence, and joy. These practices can be as simple as saying a prayer before meals or journaling about gratitude before bed.

Embracing Pleasure and Sensuality in All Aspects of Life

A transforming technique that encourages people to develop a deeper connection with themselves, others, and the world around them is to embrace pleasure and sensuality in all facets of life. Sensuality and pleasure are frequently linked to bodily experiences and feelings, such as indulging in delectable meals, unwinding with a massage, or spending quality time with a significant other. But sensuality and pleasure are much more than just physical; they also include emotional, mental, and spiritual aspects. People can access a rich source of happiness, fulfillment, and vitality as well as feel more intimate, connected, and well-being in their lives by embracing pleasure and sensuality in all facets of life.

Honoring one's own wants, preferences, and wishes while allowing oneself to feel joy, pleasure, and enjoyment in ordinary times is the fundamental component of embracing sensuality and pleasure. It entails paying attention to the body's signals and sensations and acting on what is nourishing and pleasurable at the time. This might include more luxurious activities like treating oneself to a spa day or giving in to a beloved pastime or activity, as well as more straightforward self-care practices like enjoying a warm bath, a leisurely walk in the outdoors, or a cup of tea. People can develop a more profound sense of self-awareness, self-love, and self- acceptance, as well as enjoy more ease, joy, and fulfillment by making pleasure and sensuality a priority in their daily lives.

Embracing sensuality and pleasure also entails learning to be mindful and present in daily activities so that one can completely experience and appreciate each moment as it comes to pass. This can include taking time to appreciate the small things in life, like sharing a wonderful dinner with friends, taking in a breathtaking sunset, or listening to uplifting music. People can develop a deeper appreciation for life's beauty and richness as well as a better sense of gratitude, contentment, and fulfillment in the here and now by engaging in mindfulness and presence practices.

People can discover methods to foster pleasure and sensuality in their relationships and close connections in addition to accepting pleasure and sensuality in daily encounters. Intimacy and pleasure should be prioritized in romantic relationships, new avenues for connection and communication with one's spouse should be explored, and a sacred space should be created for the investigation and expression of sensuality. People can strengthen their relationship with their spouse, improve their communication and emotional connection, and feel more fulfilled and satisfied in their partnership by cultivating a sense of intimacy and connection in their partnership.

Exploring one's own dreams, boundaries, and desires, as well as accepting one's own distinct expression of sensuality and sexuality, can all be part of embracing pleasure and sensuality. This might entail developing an openness, curiosity, and exploratory mindset in one's intimate and sexual interactions, as well as venturing into new experiences, dreams, and wants. People can develop a stronger feeling of self-acceptance, self-confidence, and self-expression, as well as more pleasure, intimacy, and fulfillment in their intimate relationships by respecting and accepting their own wishes and boundaries.

In summary, embracing sensuality and pleasure in all facets of life is a life-changing activity that encourages people to develop a closer relationship with others, themselves, and the outside environment. People can access a rich source of joy, fulfillment, and vitality and enjoy more intimacy, connection, and well-being in their lives by making pleasure and sensuality a priority in their daily lives. Adopting a more sensual and pleasurable approach to life can lead to more happiness, contentment, and connection. Some methods to do this include embracing one's own desires and boundaries, discovering new ways to connect and communicate with one's partner, and savoring life's small pleasures.

Cultivating Gratitude and Joy

Practicing appreciation and joy may have a profoundly positive impact on many facets of our lives, including our relationships, careers, and physical and mental health. Joy is the feeling of happiness, satisfaction, and fulfillment that results from practicing gratitude and enjoying life's abundance. Gratitude is the discipline of recognizing and appreciating the blessings, gifts, and opportunities that we have in our lives. We can change our attention from what is lacking or wrong to what is present and fabulous and intentionally cultivate thankfulness and joy. This will help us feel more resilient, happy, and fulfilled in life.

Fundamentally, developing thankfulness is making the time to recognize and be grateful for all of the gifts and blessings we frequently take for granted in our day-to-day existence. This can include more substantial gifts like excellent health, enduring relationships, or rewarding employment, as well as more miniature delights like a lovely sunrise, a delectable dinner, or a thoughtful act from a friend. We can deliberately foster a sense of abundance and appreciation for the richness of life, leading to greater joy and contentment, by actively searching out and honoring the numerous ways in which we are blessed.

In order to cultivate thankfulness, we must also change our viewpoint from one of scarcity to one of abundance, concentrate on our blessings rather than our shortcomings, and look for reasons to be grateful even in the face of adversity. This can entail viewing hardship as a chance for personal development, looking on the bright side of adversity, and realizing how adversity can bolster and enhance our resilience and thankfulness. Regardless of the outside world, we can enjoy more peace, contentment, and pleasure in our lives by developing an attitude of plenty and appreciation.

Cultivating pleasure is deliberately seeking out and accepting the situations, pursuits, and interpersonal connections that make us happy and fulfilled, in addition to practicing gratitude. This can involve engaging in hobbies and interests, going on trips, spending time in the great outdoors, and engaging in other fun activities. It can also entail developing a sense of wonder, curiosity, and amazement in our day-to-day lives. We may build a sense of joy that is independent of external circumstances and experience greater happiness, vitality, and significance in our lives by deliberately choosing to focus on what offers us joy and fulfillment.

Numerous physical and mental health advantages come from cultivating thankfulness and joy, such as decreased stress, worry, and sadness, strengthened immunity, and improved general well-being and quality of life. According to research, people who consistently nurture joy and express appreciation are likely to live longer, be happier, be more resilient, and feel more satisfied with their lives. They also tend to be in better physical health. We may improve our general health and well-being as well as feel more content, fulfilled, and energetic by bringing joy and thankfulness into our daily lives.

There are numerous methods to actively choose to focus on the things that bring us joy and fulfillment, practice mindfulness and presence in our daily activities, and keep a gratitude journal in which we list three things for which we are grateful each day are just a few of the ways we can cultivate gratitude and joy in our lives. By showing others how much we appreciate them, volunteering and giving back to our communities, and doing good deeds for both ourselves and other people, we can also foster joy and thankfulness. We can develop a strong sense of joy and appreciation that enhances every part of our lives and increases our level of happiness, fulfillment, and well-being by adopting these activities into our daily lives.

CHAPTER VIII

The Evolution of Sacred Sexuality

Future Trends and Possibilities

Examining probable future trends and opportunities provides an insight into the possible paths that culture, technology, and society may take in the years to come. We must think about how the forces of globalization, rapid technology growth, and cross-cultural interchange will affect our future and the opportunities and difficulties they may bring as we approach a new era. The future is complete with both promise and uncertainty, from the development of automation and artificial intelligence to the increasing effects of climate change and environmental degradation. We may start to foresee the possibilities that lie ahead and equip ourselves to handle the chances and difficulties of the future by looking at present trends and projections.

The continuous development of technology and its influence on every facet of our lives is one of the most important future trends. Technology is changing the way we live, work, and interact with the world around us. Examples of this include the widespread use of smartphones and wearable technology, as well as the creation of autonomous vehicles and smart cities. We anticipate even more rapid innovation and disruption in industries like biotechnology, renewable energy, and artificial intelligence in the upcoming years. This will open up new avenues for addressing global issues like resource scarcity and climate change, as well as for boosting productivity and improving human health.

The growing globalization and connectivity of civilization, which is being fueled by advancements in trade, transportation, and communication, is another significant development. A genuinely global economy and culture, where knowledge, resources, and ideas are freely exchanged across national boundaries, is emerging as the world grows increasingly interconnected. In an increasingly interconnected world, interconnectivity raises problems about sovereignty, inequality, and identity while also opening up new avenues for collaboration, creativity, and cross-cultural contact.

The future is being profoundly shaped by climate change and environmental degradation, as rising temperatures, harsh weather, and depletion of natural resources pose a threat to global economies, civilizations, and ecosystems. From switching to renewable energy sources and also adopting sustainable land use practices to building resilience and adaptation in vulnerable communities, addressing these issues will need audacious action and creative solutions on a local and global scale. Our ability as a global community to unite in the face of these pressing issues and build a more sustainable and just future for all will determine the fate of our planet.

One of the most positive developments for the future is the increasing recognition of the value of diversity, equity, and also inclusion in all sectors of society. People are becoming increasingly conscious of the need to eliminate oppressive and discriminatory systems and establish environments where everyone may flourish and realize their full potential as we work to create a more just and equitable world. This includes campaigns to support diversity and representation in leadership, the media, and other areas of power, as well as measures to combat systematic racism, sexism, homophobia, and also other forms of discrimination. If we embrace diversity and inclusion, we can create a future that is more fair, just, and inclusive for everyone.

In conclusion, examining prospective future trends and opportunities provides insight into the possible paths that culture, technology, and society might take in the years to come. The future is full of both promise and uncertainty, from the pressing need to address climate change and promote diversity and inclusion to the ongoing growth of technology and the expanding effects of globalization. We may start to foresee the possibilities that lie ahead and equip ourselves to handle the chances and difficulties of the future by looking at present trends and projections. In the end, it is up to us to define the future, and by uniting as a global society, we can make it more egalitarian, prosperous, and sustainable for everybody.

Global Perspectives on Sacred Sexuality

Views on holy sexuality from around the world provide a rich tapestry of customs, beliefs, and practices that cut across historical cultures, faiths, and civilizations. The idea of sacred sexuality is ingrained in the spiritual and cultural practices of many different communities worldwide, and it reflects the common human need for transcendence, closeness, and connection. Sacred sexuality has shaped our sense of sexuality, spirituality, and the divine, from ancient rituals and ceremonies to contemporary interpretations and behaviors.

Sacred sexuality is viewed in many indigenous cultures around the world as an essential and natural aspect of life, closely linked to the earth's rhythms, the cycles of nature, and the divine powers that rule the cosmos. These cultures embrace and evoke the powers of fertility, vitality, and creation through rituals and rites, and sexuality is frequently honored as a holy gift from the gods or ancestors. These rituals, which can incorporate dancing, music, storytelling, and other artistic mediums, are frequently used to establish a stronger sense of community and belonging as well as to facilitate divine connections.

Sacred sexuality was fundamental to religious and spiritual traditions in ancient Egypt, Greece, and India. Fertility gods and goddesses were worshipped in temples, and rituals were conducted to honor and please these deities. Practices like tantra, yoga, and sacred sexuality were utilized to cultivate awareness, vigor, and oneness with the divine in these civilizations, where sexuality was seen as a divine energy that could be exploited for spiritual growth and enlightenment. These customs still have an impact on how people understand holy sexuality today, encouraging people to investigate the relationship between spirituality, sexuality, and personal growth.

Sacred sexuality is frequently understood in the Judeo-Christian tradition through the prism of marriage and procreation. Sexuality is regarded as a sacred relationship between a husband and wife as well as a way to carry out the mandate to multiply and bear fruit. There are rich traditions of mysticism and esotericism within Christianity and Judaism that examine the spiritual dimensions of sexuality and the search for unity with the divine despite the Judeo-Christian tradition's historical stringent prohibitions on intercourse outside of marriage. These traditions provide alternate viewpoints on sexuality that emphasize love, intimacy, and oneness with the divine. They are frequently linked to characters like Mary Magdalene, the Song of Solomon, and the Kabbalah.

Sacred sexuality is closely linked to Eastern traditions like Buddhism, Taoism, and Hinduism. These traditions emphasize the connection of body, mind, and spirit via practices like qigong, yoga, and tantra that foster awareness, energy, and spiritual enlightenment. These traditions view sexuality as a potent force that can be exploited for spiritual and human development. Sexual energy is channeled for healing, transformation, and union with the divine through techniques including energy cultivation, meditation, and breathwork. These traditions provide a comprehensive understanding of sexuality that incorporates aspects of the physical, emotional, and spiritual realms. They place a strong emphasis on self-awareness, harmony, and balance as critical components of developing a positive and healthy connection with one's sexuality.

The idea of sacred sexuality has seen a rise in attention and investigation in the modern day as people attempt to reframe and reclaim their connection with sexuality in a society that frequently views it as shameful or taboo. The diversity and complexity of human sexuality are becoming more widely acknowledged, and there is a willingness to investigate new paradigms and possibilities for sexual expression and fulfillment. Examples of this include the emergence of neo-tantra and sacred sexuality workshops, as well as the growing acceptance of LGBTQ+ identities and relationships. The diversity of human experience must be honored and celebrated as our global society develops, and spaces, where everyone feels empowered, protected, and supported to explore and embrace their own distinctive expression of holy sexuality, must be established.

Continuing the Journey: Lifelong Learning and Growth

Maintaining the path of lifelong learning and development is crucial in the quickly evolving and more complicated world of today. Lifelong learning extends beyond formal schooling to include all facets of personal and professional growth. It involves the continuous acquisition of knowledge, skills, and experiences throughout one's life. This article will examine the value of lifelong learning as well as its advantages, drawbacks, and methods for promoting an environment that values ongoing improvement.

All throughout their lives, people must learn new things in order to adapt and thrive in a dynamic and always-shifting society. Staying resilient, competitive, and relevant in a world where economic shifts, societal transformations, and technological developments are happening at an unprecedented rate requires the capacity to learn and adapt. Through the acquisition of new skills, the updating of preexisting knowledge, and the embrace of new chances, lifelong learning empowers people to navigate change, take advantage of new opportunities, and pursue personal and professional progress throughout their lives.

Additionally, lifelong learning fosters well-being, contentment, and personal fulfillment. One can find meaning, fulfillment, and purpose in life by taking part in educational activities that are in line with their values, interests, and passions. Exploring interests, expressing creativity, and developing a sense of curiosity and wonder about the world around oneself are all made possible by lifelong learning, whether one is acquiring a new skill, hobby, or area of study. People can have more happiness, pleasure, and satisfaction in their lives if they constantly push themselves and broaden their views.

Moreover, lifelong learning develops critical thinking, problem-solving abilities, and intellectual curiosity. People can acquire new perspectives, ideas, and experiences that broaden their awareness of the world and strengthen their critical thinking, information analysis, and problem-solving skills. Lifelong learning promotes a culture of innovation, creativity, and resilience by encouraging people to examine different perspectives, question presumptions, and challenge conventional thinking. Furthermore, people may adapt and prosper in a world that is changing quickly and becoming more linked thanks to the skills and competencies acquired via lifelong learning, which are transferable across many contexts and domains.

But even with all of its advantages, lifelong learning has obstacles and difficulties that people must overcome. Prioritizing learning and development amidst the pressures of job, family, and other responsibilities can be challenging for people due to time, money, and competing priorities. In addition, fear of not measuring up, self-doubt, and impostor syndrome might prevent people from exploring new avenues and taking chances in their educational journey. Furthermore, there may be unequal or restricted access to high-quality education and learning resources, especially for disadvantaged or marginalized groups, which exacerbates already-existing inequalities and inequities in society.

Building a helpful and enabling environment that promotes and supports learning at all stages of life is crucial to overcoming these obstacles and fostering a culture of lifelong learning and growth. This involves making investments in inclusive, reasonably priced, and accessible education and training programs that provide people the chance to learn new skills and information regardless of their circumstances or experience. In addition, businesses, institutions, and communities can encourage lifelong learning by fostering an environment that is conducive to learning, allowing flexible work schedules, and offering tools and assistance for staff training and development. Furthermore, encouraging a culture of experimentation, curiosity, and constant improvement might assist people in overcoming their fear of failing and welcoming new chances for development.

In summary, people must continue their journey of lifelong learning and growth in order to adapt, flourish, and find fulfillment in a world that is changing quickly and becoming more complex. Through the pursuit of personal and professional development, updating preexisting knowledge, and gaining new skills throughout their lives, lifelong learning empowers people to effectively manage change, take advantage of new possibilities, and positively impact social, economic, and cultural outcomes. We can build a more inventive, resilient, and inclusive society where everyone has the chance to realize their full potential and also lead fulfilling lives by encouraging a culture of lifelong learning and growth.

CHAPTER IX

Exploring Sensuality and Erotic Expression

Understanding Sensuality Beyond the Physical

Sensuality beyond the physical plane involves a sophisticated investigation of human experiences that go beyond simple bodily perceptions. Although the five senses—sight, hearing, touch, taste, and smell—are frequently linked to sensuality, sensuality actually includes a broader range of emotional, psychological, and spiritual aspects that influence how we experience pleasure, closeness, and connection. In this section, we will examine the many facets of sensuality, its importance in the human experience, and strategies for developing and appreciating sensuality outside of the physical.

A vast array of experiences that appeal to our senses and produce feelings of pleasure, arousal, and satisfaction are categorized as sensual. Sensuality extends beyond the five senses—touch, taste, sight, smell, and hearing—and includes the psychological and emotional dimensions of human experience, such as vulnerability, closeness, and connection. It entails living in the present and appreciating its richness, relishing the feelings, experiences, and bonds that result from our interactions with the environment. Sensuality can be found in commonplace instances of beauty, joy, and connection, such as relishing a delectable meal, taking in a sunset, or having a meaningful chat with a loved one. It is not just restricted to romantic or sexual events.

Furthermore, sensuality contributes significantly to improving our general state of health and life satisfaction.

Through developing an enhanced consciousness and admiration of our perceptual encounters, we can access an abundant reservoir of enjoyment, happiness, and satisfaction that sustains our physical, mental, and spiritual selves. Sensuality promotes a sense of aliveness, vitality, and presence in our lives by enabling us to connect more intimately with one another, the environment around us, and ourselves. Furthermore, we can develop greater self-awareness, self-acceptance, and self-love by accepting sensuality as a necessary part of the human experience. This will enable us to live more fully and authentically in accordance with our values and desires.

Furthermore, realizing how our sensory experiences relate to our emotional, psychological, and spiritual aspects is essential to comprehending sensuality outside of the physical world. Sensuality encompasses both our internal reactions to and interpretations of the external stimuli we experience in addition to the external stimuli themselves. It entails allowing oneself to be totally present and involved in the moment as well as tuning into our feelings, desires, and intentions. We can strengthen our bonds with one another and the outside world by accepting our sensuality in this way, which will increase our sense of fulfillment, closeness, and joy in life.

Sensuality, however, might be disregarded or underestimated in a society that frequently places a higher priority on achievement, production, and material success. Many people may experience feelings of numbness, disconnection, and discontent as a result of feeling cut off from their bodies, senses, and emotions.

Furthermore, shame, guilt, and the repression of sensual sensations can be exacerbated by cultural norms and expectations surrounding gender, sexuality, and body image, which prevent people from completely embracing and expressing their desires and pleasures.

It is crucial to develop practices that support presence, mindfulness, and self-awareness in order to develop a better understanding of sensuality outside of the physical world. This could entail engaging in practices like yoga, meditation, or creative expression that support a loving and nonjudgmental relationship with our bodies, senses, and emotions. We can also develop a greater appreciation of our sensory experiences and connect with our sensual side by doing things that make us happy, fulfilled, and pleasurable. This could be going on a nature walk, doing something creative or artistic, or doing things that encourage closeness and interpersonal connections.

In conclusion, appreciating the complexity of the human experience and accepting the interdependence of our sensory, emotional, psychological, and spiritual components are essential to comprehending sensuality outside of the physical world. Through developing an enhanced consciousness and admiration of our perceptual encounters, we can access an abundant reservoir of enjoyment, happiness, and satisfaction that sustains our physical, mental, and spiritual selves. Furthermore, we can develop greater self-awareness, self-acceptance, and self-love by accepting sensuality as a necessary part of the human experience. This will enable us to live more fully and authentically in accordance with our values and desires.

Embracing Erotic Energy and Expression

A thorough investigation of human sexuality, desire, and intimacy that goes beyond accepted conventions and limits is necessary to embrace erotic energy and expression. Each person possesses erotic energy, a powerful force that encompasses all forms of sensuality, sexuality, and emotion. When welcomed and deliberately nurtured, it may be a source of vigor, creativity, and connection that enhances our lives and relationships. In this section, we will examine the meaning of erotic energy and expression, how it affects relationships and personal development, and how to accept and use this vital force in our lives.

An essential component of human nature, erotic energy is intricately linked to our mental, emotional, and spiritual health. It includes the feelings, wants, and emotions that come from our sensuality and sexuality, as well as the creative urge that pushes us to look for fulfillment, pleasure, and connection. Erotic energy is not just associated with sexual activity; rather, it permeates every part of our existence and has a tremendous impact on our emotions, ideas, and actions. It has the power to arouse our senses, stoke our passions, and carry us to new heights of self-expression and self-discovery. It is a dynamic and transformational force.

Moreover, developing a positive and meaningful relationship with ourselves and others requires embracing sensual energy and expression. Intimacy, connection, and communication in partnerships all depend on erotic energy, which offers a potent means of expressing want, passion, and love. Erotic expression may strengthen our emotional ties, promote trust and vulnerability, and improve the caliber of our relationships when it is accepted knowingly and truly. It creates a space for mutual inquiry, development, and fulfillment by enabling us to appreciate our bodies, wants, and pleasures without feeling guilty or judged.

In addition, accepting erotic expression and energy is a liberating and self-empowering act. Adopting an embrace of erotic energy enables people to regain control over their bodies, desires, and pleasures in a society that frequently reinforces shame, guilt, and suppression surrounding sexuality and desire. It is a bold act of self-acceptance and love that confirms our innate value and right to happiness, contentment, and pleasure. We can live more honestly and fully in accordance with our desires and ideals by embracing our erotic nature and overcoming cultural conventions and expectations that aim to restrict or stifle our sexual expression.

Accepting erotic energy and expression, meanwhile, can be difficult in a society that frequently stigmatizes and marginalizes sexuality and desire despite its transforming potential. Many people may experience repression, inhibition, or avoidance of their sexual urges and pleasures as a result of shame, guilt, or fear related to their erotic impulses. Furthermore, detrimental preconceptions and narratives that restrict or distort our understanding of erotic energy and expression can be perpetuated by societal norms and expectations around gender, sexuality, and relationships. This can leave people feeling confused, inadequate, or insecure.

In order to truly embrace erotic expression and energy, one must develop a feeling of self-awareness, self-acceptance, and self-love. This could entail being honest and upfront with ourselves and other people about our dreams, boundaries, and desires while also understanding them and exploring them without shame or condemnation. Furthermore, engaging in self-care, self-compassion, and self-pleasure practices can facilitate a more profound and also more meaningful connection between us and our bodies, desires, and pleasures, enabling us to more efficiently and confidently express our erotic energy.

To sum up, accepting erotic expression and energy is a potent and life-changing path toward freedom, emancipation, and self-discovery. We can access a powerful source of energy, creativity, and connection that enhances our lives and relationships by accepting our erotic nature. In addition, accepting and loving our sensual energy and expression is a self-love and acceptance gesture that confirms our intrinsic value and right to happiness, contentment, and pleasure. We can achieve new heights of intimacy, joy, and pleasure in our lives by embracing our erotic nature with courage, curiosity, and compassion. This will enable us to live more fully and authentically in accordance with our ideals and aspirations.

Practices for Deepening Sensual Connection

For those who want to build a more profound, more satisfying feeling of intimacy, pleasure, and connection in their life, practices that improve sensory connection are vital resources. The capacity to completely engage with our senses, feelings, and experiences is referred to as sensual connection. It enables us to fully appreciate the richness of the present and strengthen our bonds with one another, the world around us, and ourselves. This section will examine a range of methods and approaches to enhance the sensory connection, from exercises that foster communication and closeness to mindfulness and embodiment practices.

By developing present-moment awareness and attentiveness to our sensory experiences, mindfulness techniques lay the groundwork for strengthening our connection to our senses. Deliberately focusing our attention on our thoughts, feelings, and also sensations as they arise in the present moment without passing judgment is the practice of mindfulness. By engaging in mindfulness practices, we can learn to pay attention to the minute details of our sensory experiences, such as the flavor of food, the sensation of the wind against our skin, or the sound of birds chirping. This enables us to fully appreciate each moment and strengthen our bond with the natural world.

By establishing a stronger sense of presence and awareness and re-establishing our connection to our body, embodiment techniques are another effective means of enhancing sensual connection. Through embodiment techniques, we can fully inhabit and experience our physicality by tuning into the sensations, emotions, and rhythms of our bodies. We can engage more fully with our bodies and the feelings they hold by practicing practices like yoga, dance, and somatic meditation, which can help us develop a better sense of body awareness, acceptance, and appreciation.

Furthermore, by encouraging transparency, vulnerability, and honesty in our relationships, communication techniques are vital to the development of sensual connection. In order to communicate effectively, we must actively listen to our partners' needs and experiences and show empathy for them. We also need to convey our desires, boundaries, and also feelings in an honest and respectful manner. We may strengthen our emotional and sensual connection with our partners by creating a safe and also supportive environment in which we can explore our desires, dreams, and weaknesses. Some techniques that might help with this process include active listening, nonviolent communication, and erotic storytelling.

By encouraging trust, vulnerability, and emotional closeness in our relationships, intimacy-building activities can assist in improving sensual connection in addition to mindfulness, embodiment, and communication techniques. Engaging in techniques like eye gazing, aware touch, and sensual massage helps partners explore their boundaries and wants in a safe and consenting manner while also fostering a more profound sense of connection. Couples can improve their sexual connection, fortify their emotional ties, and create a more rewarding and gratifying relationship by routinely partaking in these activities.

Self-pleasure activities also enable people to explore and connect more deeply and intimately with their own bodies, wants, and joys, which makes them valuable instruments for strengthening sensual connections. To experience pleasure, arousal, and self-discovery, self-pleasure entails solo sexual acts like masturbation, self-touch, and erotic imagination. People can develop a greater sense of intimacy, enjoyment, and connection with themselves by putting self-pleasure first as a kind of self-care and self-love. This can improve their capacity to connect with others in close relationships.

But even though these techniques can be effective in strengthening a sensual bond, it's crucial to approach them with intention, curiosity, and agreement. It's critical to talk honestly and openly about our wants, dreams, and desires, as well as to respect our own and our partner's boundaries and limitations. In addition, it is critical to put safety, mutual respect, and trust first in all close relationships and to ask for help or direction when necessary.

To sum up, sensual connection techniques are an excellent resource for people who want to create deeper, more satisfying feelings of intimacy, pleasure, and connection in their lives. People can experience more joy, fulfillment, and satisfaction in their relationships and daily lives by practicing mindfulness, embodiment, communication, intimacy-building, and self-pleasure. These practices can help people connect deeper with themselves, their partners, and the world around them. We can reach new heights of closeness, pleasure, and connection as we develop a greater understanding and appreciation of our feelings, wants, and sensory experiences. This will profoundly and meaningfully improve our lives and relationships.

CHAPTER X

Sacred Sexuality and the Natural World

Connecting with Nature as a Source of Wisdom and Inspiration

Since the beginning of civilization, connecting with nature as a source of wisdom and inspiration has been an essential part of human existence. This is a timeless activity. Recognizing the tremendous wisdom and beauty inherent in the natural world, humanity has sought it throughout history for direction, healing, and spiritual nourishment. This section will discuss the importance of interacting with nature as a source of knowledge and inspiration, the advantages it has for our physical, mental, and emotional health, and strategies for strengthening our bond with the natural world.

For a very long time, people have looked to nature as a source of knowledge and inspiration. It provides an understanding of the rhythms of the universe, the cycles of life, and the interconnection of all living things. Indigenous societies all across the world have come to understand the value of nature as a teacher and guide, and they rely on the soil, plants, and animals to impart wisdom that informs their cultural practices, spiritual beliefs, and daily lives. Nature provides a multitude of teachings and insights that can broaden our perspective of who we are and how we relate to others and the world around us. These lessons and insights can come from the wisdom of old forests to the tranquility of mountaintops.

Furthermore, there are numerous advantages of spending time in nature for your mental, emotional, and physical health. Numerous studies have shown that spending time in nature improves mood and immune system performance, reduces stress, anxiety, and also depression, and enhances overall well-being. A haven from the stresses and diversions of contemporary life, nature offers a place for rest, introspection, and renewal. Spending time in nature, whether it be by going on a hike through a forest, tending to a garden in our backyard, or just relaxing under a tree, helps us reestablish our connection to the natural world, ourselves, and our senses, which promotes harmony, calm, and connection.

Moreover, fostering a connection with nature can stimulate human development, creativity, and inventiveness. The diversity, beauty, and tenacity of nature can pique our curiosity, excite our senses, and spark our imagination—all of which can motivate us to perceive the world from new perspectives and consider novel avenues. Nature's patterns, colors, and forms have inspired artists, writers, scientists, and intellectuals throughout history, serving as a source of inspiration, understanding, and discovery. We can access our inner creativity, intuition, and wisdom by immersing ourselves in nature's beauties. This opens our eyes to new possibilities for personal development and expression.

However, many people have lost touch with nature in today's fast-paced, technologically-driven world, which has resulted in a loss of appreciation for the natural world and its innate wisdom and beauty. People are becoming more and more cut off from the land, plants, and animals that support life on Earth as a result of urbanization, industrialization, and deforestation, which have also contributed to the destruction of natural habitats and ecosystems. A sedentary lifestyle and less time spent outside are other consequences of the rise of digital technology and screen-based entertainment, which have been linked to a number of physical and also mental health problems.

It is crucial to develop a sense of reverence, gratitude, and reciprocity towards the natural environment in order to strengthen our relationship with it as a source of wisdom and inspiration. This could entail spending more time outside and participating in outdoor pursuits that provide us with a direct connection to nature, including hiking, camping, gardening, or birdwatching. In order to develop a stronger sense of present and connection, it could also entail embracing techniques like mindfulness, meditation, or ecotherapy that assist us in tuning into the cycles of the natural world. In order to save the natural world for future generations, it is also critical to support environmental conservation and sustainability initiatives.

In conclusion, cultivating physical, mental, and emotional well-being, as well as encouraging creativity, innovation, and personal growth, all depend on establishing a connection with nature as a source of wisdom and inspiration. We can access a deep reservoir of knowledge, healing, and rejuvenation that uplifts and sustains our spirits by immersing ourselves in the beauty, diversity, and resilience of nature. A more peaceful and long-lasting relationship with the planet we call home can be fostered when we develop a deeper connection with the natural world and a stronger feeling of reverence, gratitude, and responsibility towards the Earth and all of its people.

Exploring Ecosexuality and Environmental Consciousness

Examining ecosexuality and environmental consciousness signifies a significant change in how people view and interact with nature. A word known as "ecosexuality" has recently come into use to refer to an identity or orientation that is marked by a strong emotional, spiritual, and sensual bond with the planet and all of its inhabitants. It includes a broad spectrum of behaviors and ideologies that are based on the notion of considering the earth to be a lover, companion, or source of closeness and enjoyment. This section will discuss ecosexuality, its effects on one's own and the planet's health, and methods for developing a closer bond with the earth.

Fundamentally, ecosexuality is based on the understanding that the earth is a sentient, living being deserving of awe, respect, and care. Ecosexuals see the natural world as a sacred partner with whom they have a close and mutually beneficial relationship rather than only as a resource to be used for human benefit. Love, gratitude, and reciprocity characterize this relationship, as ecosexuals strive to respect and appreciate the wealth, diversity, and beauty of the earth in all of its forms. Ecosexuality is a term used to describe a variety of behaviors that promote closeness, harmony, and communion with the natural world. These practices range from making love on the forest floor to communing with trees and rivers.

Furthermore, because ecosexuals frequently participate in actions and activism that advance social justice and ecological sustainability, ecosexuality and environmental consciousness are strongly related. Ecosexuals strive to live in harmony with nature and promote social change and environmental protection because they understand that human actions have a significant impact on the planet and its inhabitants. This could be leading a sustainable lifestyle, encouraging eco-friendly companies and projects, or being involved in environmental advocacy and activism. In order to create a more compassionate and sustainable relationship with the world we call home, people can develop a more profound feeling of connection, duty, and stewardship towards the earth and all of its inhabitants by living according to the principles of ecosexuality.

Moreover, ecosexuality invites people to discover and accept their sensual connection to the earth in all of its manifestations by challenging traditional ideas about sexuality, gender, and identity. By engaging in sensual activities like rolling in the mud, dancing beneath the stars, or taking a dip in a natural hot spring, ecosexual practices enable people to connect with the erotic energy and sensory pleasures of the natural world. Ecosexuals can recover their erotic power and agency by reclaiming their connection to the earth and developing a greater sense of embodiment, pleasure, and authenticity.

Though it provides a strong foundation for establishing a connection with the earth and promoting environmental consciousness, ecosexuality is not without its difficulties and detractors. Some people might consider ecosexuality to be insignificant or frivolous, considering it to be a cultural appropriation or "greenwashing" tactic. Some would argue that ecosexuality is only a lifestyle choice or political statement, casting doubt on its validity as an orientation or identity. Furthermore, some people may find it disrespectful or inappropriate for the sexualization of the natural world and the eroticization of environmental issues, especially those from traditional cultures and indigenous communities that regard the earth as a holy and spiritual entity.

It is crucial to approach the practice with humility, curiosity, and openness if one is to develop a closer relationship with the earth and investigate ecosexuality in a respectful and genuine manner. This could entail doing exercises like mindfulness, meditation, or ecotherapy, which train our senses to become more in sync with the cycles of the natural world and to feel more connected to it. It also entails respecting the sovereignty and holiness of the earth, seeking to have a proper relationship with the land and its inhabitants, and learning from indigenous wisdom and traditional ecological knowledge. Furthering our awareness of ecosexuality and its consequences for individual and global well-being also requires constant introspection, discussion, and self-examination.

To sum up, investigating ecosexuality and environmental consciousness presents a life-changing chance to develop a closer bond with the planet and promote a more compassionate and sustainable relationship with the world we live in. Love, appreciation, reciprocity, stewardship, and other ecosexual values allow us to access a vast wellspring of knowledge, healing, and rejuvenation that enlivens our lives and satisfies our souls. We may develop a stronger sense of connection, responsibility, and reverence towards the earth and all of its inhabitants by living according to the principles of ecosexuality in our relationships and daily lives. This will help to create a more peaceful and sustainable future for future generations.

Rituals and Practices for Nature-Based Sacred Sexuality

Sacred sexuality rituals and practices are a very spiritual and comprehensive way of fostering intimacy, pleasure, and fulfillment in our lives via connection to the natural world. For millennia, civilizations and traditions all over the world have embraced the idea of sacred sexuality, acknowledging the innate relationship that exists between sexuality, spirituality, and the natural environment. This section will discuss the importance of nature-based holy sexuality, its advantages for one's own and other people's well-being, and how we can create rituals and practices in our lives to strengthen our bond with the natural world and develop a more fulfilling and sacred view of sexuality.

Fundamentally, holy sexuality rooted in nature recognizes the Earth as a sacred and sentient entity deserving of awe, respect, and nurturing. It acknowledges the strength and wisdom innate in the natural world, as well as the interdependence of all living things. People can develop a more profound feeling of connection, presence, and intimacy in their lives and experience more joy, fulfillment, and vitality in their sexual and spiritual connections by accepting the Earth as a sacred partner and source of wisdom.

A fundamental tenet of nature-based holy sexuality is the conviction that sexual energy is a powerful force that can be used for spiritual development, healing, and transformation. Sexual energy is viewed as a potent life force in many spiritual traditions, one that may be directed and channeled to awaken higher realms of awareness and increase our capacity for love, joy, and connection. People can learn to engage with their sexual energy in a conscious and intentional way, strengthening their bonds with themselves, their partners, and the natural world by practicing tantra, Taoist sexual cultivation, or shamanic sexuality.

Furthermore, sacred space creation and intention-setting are critical components of rituals and practices for nature-based sacred sexuality, which honor and celebrate the Earth and all of its inhabitants. This could entail rituals like making an altar with elemental symbols, calling upon nature spirits or gods, or holding ceremonies to respect the Earth's rhythms and seasonal cycles. People who participate in these rituals might develop a stronger sense of reverence, gratitude, and connection to the natural world, which will improve their life' harmony, balance, and alignment.

Moreover, people are encouraged to discover and accept their sensual connection to the Earth in all of its manifestations by nature-based sacred sexuality. This could be engaging in sensual pursuits like having sex outside under the stars, taking a bath in a natural hot spring, or spending time outdoors connecting with the elements. People can access the sensuous delights and erotic energies of the natural world by honoring their connection to the Earth in this way, which enables them to feel more joy, ecstasy, and aliveness in their sexual and spiritual interactions.

Nonetheless, even while nature-based sacred sexuality presents significant chances for recovery, development, and transformation, these practices must be approached with humility, respect, and permission. In order to maintain a healthy relationship with the land, flora, fauna, and spirits that support life on Earth, it is crucial to respect the sovereignty and agency of the planet and all of its inhabitants. Furthering our awareness of nature-based holy sexuality and its implications for individual and planetary well-being requires constant self-inquiry, reflection, and discourse.

In order to integrate ceremonies and actions for nature-based sacred sexuality into our lives, we must establish a secure and encouraging environment for experimentation and discovery. Finding or developing community places where people may gather together to share their experiences, ideas, and practices in an accepting and nonjudgmental setting may be necessary to achieve this. Working with seasoned mentors, teachers, or guides who can offer direction, accountability, and support on the path of sacred sexuality may also be necessary.

To sum up, rituals and practices for nature-based sacred sexuality provide effective means of fostering intimacy, joy, and fulfillment in our lives as well as a strong connection with the Earth. People can access a tremendous amount of development, healing, and transformation that enlivens their lives and satisfies their hearts by accepting the Earth as a sacred partner and source of wisdom. We may develop a stronger sense of reverence, harmony, and connection with the Earth and all of its inhabitants by living out the principles of nature-based sacred sexuality in our daily lives and interpersonal relationships. This will promote a more holy and sustainable way of being in the world.

CHAPTER XI

Integrating Sacred Sexuality into Community and Society

Building Conscious Communities of Sacred Connection

Cultivating deeper connections with ourselves, each other, and the Earth is a transforming undertaking that goes into creating conscious communities of sacred connection. There has never been a more pressing need for genuine community and deep connections in today's fast-paced, sometimes disconnected world. Conscious communities of sacred connection offer a safe space for people to come together around a shared purpose and vision, as well as a sense of belonging and support. This section will discuss the importance of aware communities, their advantages for both individual and group well-being, and how we might develop and support them in our daily lives.

The understanding is that each and every one of us is a part of the vast and complex web of life and that connection and dependence are fundamental to conscious communities of sacred connection. These communities acknowledge our shared responsibility to care for one another and the planet while also seeking to honor and celebrate the inherent worth and dignity of each human. Conscious communities foster a feeling of inclusivity and belonging, giving people a platform to express their unique talents, discover their true selves, and advance society.

Additionally, intentional communities of holy connection provide a nurturing atmosphere for development, recovery, and metamorphosis. People can obtain support, motivation, and direction from one another when they unite around a common goal and objective, which promotes higher states of self-awareness, self- acceptance, and self-expression. Members of conscious communities can confront their fears and limitations, explore their inner landscapes, and develop greater resilience, compassion, and empathy in their lives through activities including meditation, ritual, and group discussion.

Moreover, a sense of connection and belonging to the Earth and all its people is greatly enhanced by conscious communities of holy connection. These communities strive to live in harmony with nature and promote social justice and environmental protection. They acknowledge the Earth as a sacred companion and source of wisdom. Earth-based rituals, eco-activism, and sustainable living are among the practices that members of conscious communities can engage in to strengthen their bond with the natural world and support the healing and regeneration of the planet.

Nevertheless, there are difficulties and complexity involved in creating conscious communities of sacred connection. It can be challenging to foster genuine community and meaningful connections in a culture that frequently places a higher value on independence, competition, and materialism. Furthermore, resolving internal conflicts, power dynamics, diversity, and inclusivity challenges among conscious communities calls for constant communication, introspection, and teamwork. Furthermore, conscious communities may encounter outside forces and barriers like economic downturns, legal limitations, or societal shame that call for tenacity, inventiveness, and persistence to overcome.

Establishing a secure and encouraging environment for investigation and development is crucial to the development of conscious communities of holy connection. This could entail creating unambiguous rules, guidelines, and procedures for interaction and dispute resolution in addition to encouraging an environment where members respect, trust, and assist one another. In order to acknowledge and appreciate each person's unique gifts and contributions, as well as to strengthen the community's links and shared ideals, it may also entail providing chances for shared rituals, ceremonies, and celebrations.

Furthermore, diversity, inclusion, and equity must be given top priority by aware communities in all facets of their operations and decision-making procedures. This could entail actively seeking out and elevating the voices and perspectives of the underprivileged, as well as resolving any systematic injustices and hurdles that the community may have. Conscious communities may create a space where everyone feels seen, heard, and respected and where they can all offer their unique skills and abilities to the greater good by cultivating a culture of openness, inquiry, and humility.

To sum up, creating conscious communities of sacred connection presents a significant chance to foster closer ties to the Earth, one another, and ourselves. People can establish a space where they can explore their authentic selves, assist one another in personal growth and change, and contribute to the healing and regeneration of the Earth by uniting in common purpose and intention. We may access a tremendous wellspring of fortitude, creativity, and fortitude that uplifts and nourishes our souls as we create conscious communities of sacred connection in our lives.

Sacred Sexuality and Social Change

Sacred sexuality and social change are related spheres of human experience that can significantly alter people's lives, relationships, and communities. Viewing sexuality as a potent force for healing, transformation, and spiritual growth, sacred sexuality is based on both current holistic techniques and ancient spiritual traditions. It acknowledges the innate holiness of the human body, sensual energy, and intimate connection. On the other side, social reform entails a group effort to solve structural inequities, advance equality and justice, and build a society that is more caring and just for everyone. In this section, we will examine the relationship between holy sexuality and social change, as well as how it can spur individual and group transformation and how communities might use sacred sexuality to advance positive social change.

Fundamentally, holy sexuality celebrates the innate sacredness of sensual energy and close connection while acknowledging the interdependence of the body, mind, and spirit. It entails techniques like shamanic sexuality, tantra, and Taoist sexual cultivation that encourage people to deliberately and consciously explore and accept their erotic energy in order to strengthen their bonds with the divine, their relationships, and themselves. People can access a significant source of healing, joy, and spiritual awakening by developing a deeper awareness and acceptance of their sexuality. They may experience new degrees of closeness, fulfillment, and connection as a result.

Furthermore, sacred sexuality can serve as a catalyst for development in relationships and in individuals, resulting in higher levels of empowerment, authenticity, and self-awareness. People can develop more profound degrees of intimacy, trust, and connection with their partners by practicing techniques like mindful touch, conscious communication, and erotic rituals. This will increase their level of joy, pleasure, and fulfillment in their relationships. Furthermore, holy sexuality empowers people to rediscover their agency and erotic power by allowing them to safely and consensually explore and embrace their boundaries, dreams, and desires.

Moreover, by questioning prevailing narratives and norms regarding sexuality, gender, and relationships and advocating for more inclusive, egalitarian, and compassionate ways of being in the world, holy sexuality has the capacity to spark good social change. People can fight to undermine oppressive and unequal structures that support sexual assault, discrimination, and stigma by adopting the holy sexuality principles of consent, pleasure, and connection. Furthermore, holy sexuality may be a potent weapon for advancing the rights and health of sexual and reproductive processes, including the destigmatization of various sexual identities and orientations, access to abortion and contraception, and comprehensive sex education.

Nevertheless, sacred sexuality is not without its difficulties and complexity, even while it has the capacity to spark constructive societal transformation. It can be difficult and even dangerous to embrace holy sexuality and challenge prevailing conventions surrounding sexuality in a society that frequently places a higher value on independence, competition, and consumerism. Furthermore, specific individuals or organizations that feel threatened by the concept of sexual emancipation, autonomy, and empowerment may oppose or react negatively against sacred sexuality. Furthermore, holy sexuality can interact with other oppressions like racism, sexism, homophobia, and transphobia, which makes it harder for oppressed communities to access and develop their agency and erotic power.

In all facets of our individual and communal lives, we must foster a culture of permission, respect, and inclusivity if we are to utilize the power of holy sexuality for social change fully. In addition to pushing for laws and procedures that support everyone's rights to sexual and reproductive health, this may entail providing safe and encouraging environments where people can explore and express their sexuality without feeling judged, ashamed, or afraid. Furthermore, it is critical that we prioritize the needs, goals, and viewpoints of underrepresented communities in our attempts to bring about constructive social change. This includes amplifying the voices and experiences of people who have historically been marginalized or silenced.

To sum up, holy sexuality and social change are related facets of the human experience that have the power to alter people's lives, relationships, and communities drastically. People and communities may build a more just, equitable, and compassionate society for all by embracing the sacred sexuality's tenets of consent, pleasure, and connection, as well as striving to topple oppressive and unequal systems. By utilizing holy sexuality to effect positive social change, we can access a deep wellspring of healing, pleasure, and emancipation that elevates our existence and replenishes our souls.

Empowering Individuals and Relationships within Larger Systems

Recognizing and addressing the interconnection of personal, relational, and societal processes is a multidimensional activity that aims to empower individuals and relationships within larger systems. Fundamentally, empowerment is about giving people and communities a sense of agency, autonomy, and self-determination so they can navigate and have an impact on the systems in which they live and work. This section will discuss the value of empowering people and relationships within more extensive systems, as well as the difficulties and obstacles that come with it. It will also discuss tactics for encouraging higher degrees of autonomy, agency, and resilience in the face of systemic difficulties.

Acknowledging each person's intrinsic value and dignity, as well as their distinct identities, experiences, and viewpoints, is the first step toward empowerment. It entails giving people the chance to grow in their capacities for self-awareness, self-efficacy, and self-confidence, as well as to acquire the knowledge, tools, and support systems necessary for their success. Fostering a culture of cooperation, mutual respect, and trust in interpersonal interactions and communities is another aspect of empowerment that enables people to work together toward shared objectives.

In addition, empowerment entails tackling the structural obstacles and disparities that restrict people's and communities' access to opportunities, resources, and decision-making authority. This may entail combating oppressive and discriminatory structures that uphold injustices and marginalization, such as ableism, homophobia, sexism, and racism. It could also entail promoting laws and procedures that uphold inclusivity, equity, and social justice, as well as dealing with the underlying causes of structural inequities.

Empowerment also entails realizing how interpersonal, social, and societal dynamics are interwoven and how decisions and actions made by one individual can have a cascading effect on broader systems. This necessitates that people accept accountability for their own attitudes, sentiments, and actions, as well as acknowledge their influence on the environment. It also calls on people to develop compassion, empathy, and a sense of solidarity with others, as well as to collaborate to achieve shared objectives.

However, there are difficulties and complications involved in empowering people and relationships inside more extensive systems. It frequently takes a persistent effort and group effort to eliminate systemic barriers and disparities since they are firmly ingrained and difficult to change. Individuals may also encounter internal obstacles that restrict their capacity to speak up for others and themselves, such as fear, self-doubt, and learned helplessness. In addition, communities and individuals may encounter outside obstacles that limit their capacity to fully engage and prosper in society, such as a lack of resources, social shame, or legal limitations.

Establishing supportive settings and mechanisms that value the contributions and viewpoints of all people and communities is crucial to promoting empowerment within more extensive systems. Creating possibilities for meaningful involvement and decision-making in all spheres of life, such as governance, healthcare, work, and education, maybe one way to achieve this. It also entails giving people access to networks of support, resources, and services that enable them to realize their dreams and ambitions. In order to solve systemic problems and inequality, it is also critical to foster education and awareness of them, as well as to continue working together and having ongoing conversations.

Furthermore, promoting empowerment within more expansive institutions necessitates a dedication to social justice, equity, and inclusion, as well as a readiness to confront oppressive and discriminatory systems wherever they are found. This could entail launching grassroots campaigns, promoting policy reforms, or taking direct action to combat structural inequalities and advance constructive social change. In order to prioritize the needs, goals, and viewpoints of underrepresented communities in decision-making processes may also entail elevating their voices and experiences.

In summary, strengthening people and relationships within larger systems is an important project that calls for a dedication to social justice, equity, and inclusion, as well as an understanding of the interconnection of personal, relational, and societal dynamics. People and communities can develop higher degrees of agency, autonomy, and resilience in the face of systemic problems by addressing systemic barriers and inequalities and by promoting a culture of cooperation, trust, and mutual respect. We can make the world more fair, compassionate, and just for everyone if we cooperate to strengthen bonds between people and within more extensive systems.

CHAPTER XII

Embracing Pleasure: The Art of Sensual Exploration

Cultivating a Mindful Approach to Pleasure

By bringing conscious awareness and intention to our pleasure experiences, we may fully taste and appreciate the richness and depth of life's sensory delights. This is what it means to cultivate a thoughtful approach to pleasure. Developing mindfulness in our attitude to pleasure can provide a potent counterbalance to stress, worry, and unhappiness, enabling us to feel greater joy, fulfillment, and presence in our lives in a culture that frequently promotes productivity, achievement, and rapid gratification. We will talk about the value of cultivating a thoughtful attitude toward pleasure, its benefits for relationships and our own well-being, and how to apply mindfulness to our daily lives in order to increase our emotions of fulfillment and pleasure.

Fundamentally, mindfulness means being fully present in the moment with curiosity, openness, and lack of judgment. This allows us to interact fully with our experiences without getting sidetracked or distracted by ideas, feelings, or other distractions. By using mindfulness in our pleasurable experiences, we can completely taste and appreciate the richness and depth of our experiences by applying heightened awareness and sensitivity to the sensations, emotions, and ideas that arise. We may become more aware of our bodies, preferences, and desires by practicing mindfulness when it comes to pleasure. This will enable us to make more deliberate and attentive decisions about how we look for and enjoy pleasure in our lives.

Furthermore, developing a mindful approach to pleasure has several advantages for our mental, emotional, and physical health. By bringing conscious awareness and presence to our pleasure experiences, we can enhance our capacity to feel joy, pleasure, and satisfaction in the here and now, no matter what the external circumstances may be. Moreover, mindfulness can help us become more self-aware and accept who we are, enabling us to accept and value our bodies, desires, and preferences without feeling guilty or judged. Furthermore, practicing mindfulness can help us develop more muscular emotional control and resilience, which will enable us to deal with obstacles and disappointments more calmly and efficiently.

In addition, developing a thoughtful attitude to pleasure can improve our interpersonal connections and relationships, enabling us to strengthen our bonds of intimacy, trust, and affection with our friends, family, and significant others. We can develop better empathy, compassion, and understanding by bringing conscious awareness and presence to our interactions and pleasurable experiences with others. This will enable us to genuinely perceive and appreciate the distinctive characteristics and viewpoints of those around us. By encouraging open conversation, respect for one another, and emotional awareness, mindfulness can also assist us in building more robust and more satisfying relationships. This will enable us to handle disagreements and obstacles more skillfully and gracefully.

Developing a conscious approach to pleasure is challenging, though. A culture that frequently encourages excess, hedonism, and quick gratification makes it challenging to cultivate awareness of our approach to pleasure; it takes time, effort, and patience. Furthermore, people may encounter psychological obstacles that prevent them from completely embracing and appreciating their sensations of pleasure, such as guilt, shame, or unfavorable ideas about pleasure. In addition, people may encounter outside obstacles that limit their capacity to look for and enjoy pleasure in gratifying and healthful ways, such as legal constraints, cultural standards, or social stigma.

It is imperative that we exercise self-awareness, self-compassion, and self-care in order to develop a thoughtful attitude to pleasure. We must also allow ourselves to explore and appreciate our desires, preferences, and boundaries with kindness and curiosity. This could entail engaging in techniques like mindfulness, meditation, or body-centered therapy, which support us in being more accepting and conscious of our bodies, feelings, and emotions. In order to increase our repertoire of enjoyable experiences and foster better happiness and contentment in our lives, it may also entail trying out new things that make us happy, fulfilled, and joyful.

In addition, developing a culture of permission, respect, and communication in our interpersonal connections and interactions is a crucial part of taking a mindful approach to pleasure because it enables us to value and respect the autonomy, agency, and limits of others around us. This could entail carefully listening to and respecting our partners' and friends' needs and preferences, as well as having candid discussions with them about our expectations, boundaries, and goals. It might also entail using affirmative communication and active consent in our intimate relationships and sexual interactions, which enables us to create more secure and civilized environments for expressing and exploring our fantasies and desires.

To sum up, developing a mindful attitude to pleasure presents a life-changing chance to strengthen our bonds with one another, the world, and ourselves. This enables us to live more joyful, fulfilled, and present moments. We can thoroughly enjoy and appreciate the richness and depth of life's sensory joys by bringing conscious awareness and intention to our experiences of pleasure. This enables us to build greater fulfillment and contentment in our lives. By practicing mindfulness in our enjoyment of pleasure, we can access a deep wellspring of joy, healing, and connection that elevates and replenishes our spirits.

Exploring Sensory Awakening and Erotic Play

Examining sensory awakening and erotic play invites us to investigate the entire spectrum of feelings, pleasures, and opportunities accessible to us as sensual beings. It is a voyage into the depths of our sensory experiences and erotic desires. In order to appropriately interact with our surroundings and experiences, sensory awakening entails arousing our senses—sight, hearing, touch, taste, and smell—to the richness and beauty of the world around us. In contrast, erotic play enables us to access the transforming potential of pleasure and intimacy by means of playful and consensual exploration and expression of our erotic desires, fantasies, and boundaries. This section will discuss the importance of investigating sensory awakening and erotic play, the advantages they present for relationships and personal development, and how to incorporate them into our daily lives to improve our feelings of pleasure and closeness.

In order to completely immerse oneself in the richness and depth of the present moment, sensory awakening entails bringing conscious awareness and presence to our sensory experiences. This could entail engaging in techniques that foster a deeper awareness and appreciation of our senses and sensations, such as mindfulness meditation, sensory exploration, or sensory deprivation. We can feel more joy, wonder, and aliveness in our lives by expanding our senses and strengthening our bonds with one another and the environment.

Investigating sensory awakening can also be very beneficial to our mental, emotional, and physical health. No matter what is going on outside of us, we may improve our ability to feel joy, happiness, and pleasure in the here and now by practicing mindful awareness and presence with our senses. In addition to fostering more self-acceptance and self-awareness, sensory awakening enables us to accept and value our bodies, wants, and preferences without feeling guilty or judged. Furthermore, sensory awakening can support us in developing more substantial emotional control and resilience, which will enable us to deal with obstacles and disappointments more calmly and efficiently.

Exploring erotic play also entails embracing our imaginations, boundaries, and erotic needs in a playful and consenting way, which enables us to access the transformational potential of closeness and pleasure. Depending on personal tastes and comfort levels, sexual play can encompass anything from sensual massage and erotic storytelling to role-playing and BDSM. We can experience more closeness, trust, and connection in our relationships by investigating erotic play and strengthening our bonds with ourselves and our partners.

Nevertheless, there are difficulties and complications involved in investigating sensory awakening and sensual play. Exploring our sensual impulses and fantasies can be difficult and even dangerous in a society that frequently stigmatizes and shames sexuality. It requires courage, vulnerability, and self-awareness. Furthermore, people may have psychological obstacles that prevent them from fully embracing and expressing their erotic urges, such as guilt, shame, or unfavorable views about sexuality. In addition, people may encounter outside obstacles that limit their capacity to explore and express their sexuality in satisfying and healthful ways, such as legal limits, cultural standards, or societal stigma.

It is vital to develop an attitude of curiosity, openness, and playfulness in our relationship with our senses and sexuality in order to investigate sensory awakening and erotic play. This could include doing things that make us happy, excited, or pleasurable so that we can explore and express our imaginations and desires in a safe and consenting way. It might also entail fostering an atmosphere of acceptance and experimentation where people can express themselves freely and honestly without worrying about being judged or ashamed.

Furthermore, consent, trust, and open communication are necessary when investigating sensory awakening and erotic play in our relationships and interactions with others. This could entail carefully listening to and respecting our partners' and friends' needs and preferences, as well as having candid discussions with them about our expectations, boundaries, and goals. It might also entail using affirmative communication and active consent in our intimate relationships and sexual interactions, which enables us to create more secure and civilized environments for expressing and exploring our fantasies and desires.

To sum up, investigating sensory awakening and erotic play presents a life-changing chance to strengthen our bonds with one another and the outside world, allowing us to lead happier, more contented lives. We may thoroughly enjoy and appreciate the richness and depth of life's sensory delights by bringing conscious awareness and presence to our sensory experiences and sensual urges. This enables us to build deeper fulfillment and connection in our lives. By delving into sensory awakening and sensual play, we can access a deep wellspring of pleasure, healing, and connection that nourishes and enhances our lives.

Honoring the Sacredness of Pleasure in Intimate Connections

Recognizing and appreciating the extraordinary beauty and significance of pleasure in the context of our closest relationships is a necessary step in upholding the sacredness of pleasure in intimate ties. It means treating pleasure with honor, deference, and awareness so that it might lead to more intimate relationships and spiritual development. This section will discuss the value of recognizing the sanctity of pleasure in close relationships, the advantages it provides for one's own and other people's well-being, and strategies for developing a more conscious and sacred approach to pleasure in our personal relationships.

Fundamentally, appreciating the sacredness of pleasure in close relationships means seeing pleasure to be a gift from God, an embodiment of the divine in both ourselves and our partners. It means treating everyone with love, compassion, and respect and appreciating their intrinsic value and dignity as well as their preferences, boundaries, and desires. We can learn to appreciate the beauty even more. and richness of our sensory experiences by approaching pleasure with reverence and awareness. This will enable us to truly taste and appreciate the gift of pleasure in our close relationships.

Respecting the sacredness of pleasure in close relationships also has many positive effects on one's own and other people's well-being. We can strengthen our bonds with the divine, our partners, and ourselves by developing a more thoughtful and reverent approach to pleasure. This will enable us to enjoy more joy, fulfillment, and spiritual development in our relationships. Along with helping us to let go of stress, tension, and trauma, pleasure may also be a potent healing and transformation tool. It can help us develop better resilience, energy, and well-being in our lives.

In addition, fostering an environment that is encouraging and nurturing for experimentation and expression is another way to respect the sacredness of pleasure in close relationships. It means cultivating open lines of communication, mutual respect, and trust in our relationships so that we may honestly and authentically negotiate our dreams, boundaries, and desires. We may empower ourselves and our partners to completely accept and enjoy our erotic needs and fantasies, enabling them to be a source of intimacy, joy, and connection in our relationships.This can be accomplished by offering a safe space free from bias where people can explore and express themselves.

Respecting the sanctity of pleasure in close relationships is not without difficulties, though. Accepting pleasure as sacred can be tricky, even taboo, in a society that frequently stigmatizes and shames sexuality. It calls for bravery, vulnerability, and self-awareness. Furthermore, people may have psychological obstacles that prevent them from fully embracing and expressing their dreams and wants, such as shame, remorse, or unfavorable views about pleasure. In addition, people may encounter outside obstacles that limit their capacity to explore and express their sexuality in satisfying and healthful ways, such as legal limits, cultural standards, or societal stigma.

In our relationships and interactions with others, we must foster a culture of permission, respect, and communication in order to recognize the sacredness of pleasure in close connections. This could entail carefully listening to and respecting our partners' and friends' needs and preferences, as well as having candid discussions with them about our expectations, boundaries, and goals. It might also entail using affirmative communication and active consent in our intimate relationships and sexual interactions, which enables us to create more secure and civilized environments for expressing and exploring our fantasies and desires.

Furthermore, in order to respect the sanctity of pleasure in close relationships, we must make a commitment to self-awareness, self-compassion, and self-care. This enables us to accept and explore our limits, preferences, and desires with kindness and curiosity. This could entail engaging in techniques like mindfulness, meditation, or body-centered therapy, which support us in being more accepting and conscious of our bodies, feelings, and emotions. In order to increase our repertoire of enjoyable experiences and foster greater happiness and contentment in our lives, it may also entail trying out new things that make us happy, joyful, or fulfilled.

To sum up, recognizing the sacredness of pleasure in close relationships provides a life-changing chance to strengthen our bonds with the divine, our partners, and ourselves. This enables us to enjoy more joy, fulfillment, and spiritual development in our relationships. Our appreciation of the beauty can grow. and richness of our sensory experiences by treating pleasure with reverence, respect, and mindfulness. This will enable us to completely taste and appreciate the gift of pleasure in our close relationships. We can access a vast reservoir of joy, healing, and connection that uplifts and sustains our spirits when we respect the sacredness of pleasure in our relationships.

CHAPTER XIII

The Path Forward: Embodying Sacred Sexuality

Integration and Application of Learnings

Recognizing, valuing, and appreciating the great significance of pleasure in the context of our closest relationships is necessary to honor the sacredness of pleasure in intimate relationships. It entails treating pleasure as a sacred gift that can strengthen our bonds with the divine, our partners, and ourselves. We must approach pleasure with reverence, attention, and respect. This section will examine the various aspects of respecting the sacredness of pleasure in close relationships. It will also examine the spiritual, emotional, and relational significance of pleasure as well as valuable strategies for developing a more mindful and sacred attitude toward pleasure in our relationships.

To truly respect the sacredness of pleasure in close relationships, one must see pleasure as a transformative and sacred power, an embodiment of the divine in both oneself and one's partner. It is about treating each person with love, compassion, and reverence in recognition of their intrinsic value and dignity—their choices, boundaries, and desires. We can better appreciate the richness and beauty of our sensory experiences by approaching pleasure with awareness and intention. This will enable us to completely appreciate and cherish the gift of pleasure in our close relationships.

The understanding that pleasure is more than just a bodily experience and can lead to greater intimacy, connection, and spiritual development is the foundation of the path toward appreciating the sacredness of pleasure in close relationships. Pleasure, when treated with respect and awareness, maybe a potent catalyst for change in both our personal and interpersonal lives, bringing us closer to our spiritual selves and experiencing more joy, fulfillment, and spiritual connection with others. When we accept pleasure as sacred, we open the door for it to become a tool for empowerment, liberation, and healing. This helps us let go of past traumas, wounds, and conditioning that could have prevented us from completely embracing and celebrating our erotic selves.

Furthermore, recognizing the sanctity of pleasure in close relationships encourages us to establish a safe space for experimentation and expression. Order to negotiate our desires, boundaries, and fantasies with honesty and sincerity requires us to build clear communication, trust, and mutual respect in our relationships. We enable ourselves and our partners to fully accept and enjoy our erotic needs and dreams, enabling them to be a source of intimacy, joy, and connection in our relationships by cultivating a culture of consent, respect, and communication.

Respecting the sanctity of pleasure in close relationships is not without difficulties, though. Adopting a sacred view of pleasure in a society that frequently stigmatizes and shames sexuality can encounter opposition or condemnation, necessitating bravery, vulnerability, and self-awareness. Furthermore, people may have psychological obstacles that prevent them from fully embracing and expressing their dreams and wants, such as shame, remorse, or unfavorable views about pleasure. Furthermore, extrinsic obstacles like cultural norms, legal constraints, or social stigma may make it more difficult for them to explore and express their sexuality in ways that are gratifying and healthy.

In our relationships and interactions with others, we must foster a culture of permission, respect, and communication in order to recognize the sacredness of pleasure in close connections. This could entail carefully listening to and respecting our partners' and friends' needs and preferences, as well as having candid discussions with them about our expectations, boundaries, and goals. It might also entail using affirmative communication and active consent in our intimate relationships and sexual interactions, which enables us to create more secure and civilized environments for expressing and exploring our fantasies and desires.

Furthermore, in order to respect the sanctity of pleasure in close relationships, we must make a commitment to self-awareness, self-compassion, and self-care. This enables us to accept and explore our limits, preferences, and desires with kindness and curiosity. This could entail engaging in techniques like mindfulness, meditation, or body-centered therapy, which support us in being more accepting and conscious of our bodies, feelings, and emotions. In order to increase our repertoire of enjoyable experiences and foster greater happiness and contentment in our lives, it may also entail trying out new things that make us happy, joyful, or fulfilled.

To sum up, recognizing the sacredness of pleasure in close relationships provides a life-changing chance to strengthen our bonds with the divine, our partners, and ourselves. This enables us to enjoy more joy, fulfillment, and spiritual development in our relationships. Treating pleasure with regard, respect, and mindfulness can help us appreciate the beauty and also richness of our sensory experiences on a deeper level. This will enable us to truly relish and cherish the gift of pleasure in our close relationships. We can access a vast reservoir of joy, healing, and connection that uplifts and sustains our spirits when we respect the sacredness of pleasure in our relationships.

Sustaining and Nurturing Sacred Connections

Understanding our own and others' innate divinity is the foundation of maintaining and fostering meaningful ties. It entails appreciating and respecting the sanctity of every person's distinct essence and realizing that we are all entwined and a part of a more excellent cosmic web of existence. We can make room for the divine to emerge and grow in our relationships by treating them with care and respect. This enables us to connect intimately and find more fulfillment in our connections with others.

Furthermore, it takes a dedication to open-heartedness, vulnerability, and sincerity in our interactions to maintain and nurture sacred connections. It means letting ourselves be seen, heard, and respected for who we really are by fully and truthfully expressing ourselves. Deeper intimacy and connection can arise when we foster an atmosphere of openness and vulnerability in our interactions. This enables us to build relationships that are founded on mutual respect, trust, and authenticity.

However, maintaining and fostering sacred relationships has its challenges. Building solid and meaningful relationships can be complicated in a society that frequently places a higher value on individualism, rivalry, and self-interest. Furthermore, people may experience psychological obstacles that prevent them from thoroughly engaging and connecting with others, such as fear of vulnerability, abandonment, or rejection. Furthermore, external obstacles like societal conventions, cultural expectations, or institutional inequities could make it more difficult for them to establish and preserve deep relationships with other people.

Cultivating practices that strengthen and expand our relationships with ourselves, others, and the environment around us is crucial to maintaining and nurturing sacred connections. This may entail engaging in techniques like self-reflection, mindfulness, or meditation that support us in developing higher levels of self-awareness and self-compassion, which enables us to establish stronger connections with our own inner wisdom and intuition. It also entails exercises in compassion, understanding, and thankfulness that foster closer relationships with people and enable us to recognize and value the innate divinity in every person we come into contact with.

Furthermore, maintaining and fostering sacred connections calls for emotional intelligence, mutual respect, and open communication in our partnerships.

This could entail actively listening to and supporting the experiences of our spouses, friends, and loved ones, as well as having candid discussions with them about our needs, wants, and boundaries. Furthermore, it could entail exhibiting empathy and compassion in our relationships, enabling us to encourage and assist others on their path to self-awareness and development.

Additionally, maintaining and fostering holy connections entails fostering an atmosphere that is encouraging and supportive of development and transformation. To enable people to freely explore and express themselves without fear of rejection or judgment means cultivating a culture of trust, authenticity, and non-judgment in our relationships. By establishing a secure and encouraging environment for learning and development, we enable both ourselves and other people to develop more intimate, fulfilling, and connected connections.

In summary, maintaining and fostering holy relationships calls for commitment, deliberateness, and practice. It is a lifelong process. Deeper connection, closeness, and fulfillment in our relationships can arise when we acknowledge and respect the innate divinity in each other and ourselves. We may create relationships based on mutual respect, trust, and understanding by practicing authenticity, vulnerability, and open-heartedness. We can access a rich reservoir of healing, development, and metamorphosis that enlivens our existence and satisfies our souls as we proceed on our path of maintaining and fostering holy connections.

Contributions to Personal and Collective Transformation

"Contributions to Personal and Collective Transformation" examines the various ways in which people and communities support the development, evolution, and positive transformation of both the individual and the group. It explores the connections between individual and group development, emphasizing the role that social dynamics, cultural transformations, and personal agency have in promoting significant and long-lasting change. This section will examine the different aspects of human and group transformation, the causes behind their existence, and workable methods for promoting development and constructive change on a personal and social level.

Profound changes in awareness, conduct, and identity result from the process of inner development, self-actualization, and self-discovery that characterizes personal transformation. It encompasses a wide range of pursuits and encounters, including self-examination and introspection, personal development, and spiritual awakening. Deep unhappiness or alienation from one's current way of being is often the catalyst for personal transformation, leading individuals to set out on a path of self-discovery and personal development. People can develop greater self-awareness, self-acceptance, and self-empowerment through techniques like mindfulness, meditation, therapy, or self-help. This enables them to let go of outdated thought patterns, conditioning, and habits that no longer serve them and to embrace fresh approaches to feeling, thinking, and being.

Conversely, collective transformation entails a process of institutional, social, and cultural change that results in changes to societal norms, values, and behaviors. It includes a broad spectrum of activities, campaigns, and projects that seek to promote social equality, solve structural inequities, and enhance well-being among all. Understanding the interconnectedness of all beings and having a strong feeling of empathy and compassion for others are frequently the first steps toward collective development. People can cooperate to confront oppressive institutions, demolish unfair structures, and build more inclusive, egalitarian, and sustainable communities through activism, advocacy, and collective action.

Furthermore, there is a strong correlation between individual and group development, as both processes are mutually supportive and have a profoundly transformational effect on one another. Individuals who undergo personal transformation are frequently motivated to become agents of social change and to work for a more equitable, compassionate, and sustainable world. This serves as a catalyst for collective change. On the other hand, group change can foster the circumstances and chances for individual development and self-realization, giving people the networks, resources, and assistance they require to develop higher levels of agency, self-awareness, and empowerment.

However, there are difficulties and barriers associated with both individual and group transformation. Personal transformation might encounter opposition or skepticism in a society that frequently values materialism, competition, and individuality. This is because it requires people to get over cultural norms and societal conditioning that may prevent them from completely embracing and expressing who they really are. Similar to individual hurdles, power disparities and ingrained interests that aim to uphold the status quo and oppose change can impede collective development. Furthermore, people may have internal obstacles like fear, doubt, or uncertainty that prevent them from taking part in group activities and bringing about social change.

It is imperative that we and others develop a sense of agency, empowerment, and resilience in order to promote both individual and group transformation. This may entail engaging in activities like self-care, self-compassion, and self-reflection that support the development of more self-awareness, self-acceptance, and self-empowerment and enable us to face obstacles and disappointments with more grace and calm. It also entails creating caring and encouraging communities that give people the tools, connections, and support they need to achieve their ambitions.

Furthermore, in order to create more equitable, compassionate, and sustainable societies for all living things, cultivating individual and group transformation necessitates a dedication to social justice, equity, and inclusion. This could entail opposing repressive institutions, tearing down unfair systems, and pushing for laws and procedures that uphold human dignity and social equality. Our contact with others also entails cultivating empathy, compassion, and solidarity, which enables us to forge understanding and collaboration beyond barriers of difference and division.

A strong feeling of duty and concern for the welfare of the earth and all of its inhabitants, as well as an understanding of the interconnectedness of all beings, are also necessary for promoting both individual and group transformation. A more profound connection with ourselves, others, and the natural world can be cultivated through practicing mindfulness, gratitude, and reverence for life. This enables us to acknowledge the sacredness and interconnectedness of all beings and to act wisely and compassionately in our interactions with others.

To sum up, both individual and group transformation are interrelated processes with the power to significantly and permanently alter our lives, the lives of others around us, and the environment itself. We can promote personal development and self-realization via the practice of self-awareness, empowerment, and resilience. This will enable us to serve as change agents in society. Together, we can confront oppressive institutions, demolish unfair structures, and build more just, egalitarian, and sustainable communities in order to establish a world that upholds the intrinsic value and dignity of every living thing and promotes greater well-being and flourishing for all.

CONCLUSION

Upon arriving at the conclusion of "Sacred Sexuality: Integrating Magic into Intimate Connections," I feel a profound sense of appreciation and awe for the path we have traveled together. We have examined the many facets of sacred sexuality in these pages, learning about its transformational potential, valuable uses, and lengthy history.

During our investigation, we have come across old wisdom traditions that have long honored sexual energy as a means of achieving spiritual enlightenment and unity with the divine. When we approach intimacy with mindfulness, compassion, and appreciation for the sacredness inherent in every moment of connection, we see the amazing healing that may occur.

The idea of magic—a power that exists outside the realm of reason and imbues our close interactions with awe, mystery, and profound transformation—has been central to our investigation. We have discovered how to develop an awareness of this delicate yet powerful energy via the practice of sacred sexuality, and we can use it to lead us to new heights of intimacy, connection, and spiritual development.

As we draw to a close, it is critical to recognize that the discovery of holy sexuality is a continuous and dynamic process. Every interaction presents a chance for development, education, and self-discovery. Whether we are strengthening our bond with a partner or using solo techniques to explore our sexuality, we always approach every interaction with openness, curiosity, and reverence for the beauty that resides inside.

The methods and ideas in this book will inspire, direct, and assist you as you work through the challenges of intimacy and relationships in your own life. May you always see the holiness of sexuality in all its manifestations and come to understand the power that each close relationship holds.

I hope and pray that your path to holy sexuality is one of love, joy, and profound transformation. May you never forget that the trip itself holds the natural beauty of intimacy rather than the final destination.

Thank you for buying and reading/ listening to our book. If you found this book useful/ helpful please take a few minutes and leave a review on the platform where you purchased our book. Your feedback matters greatly to us.